My Colouring Book

STRESS RELIEVE COLOURING

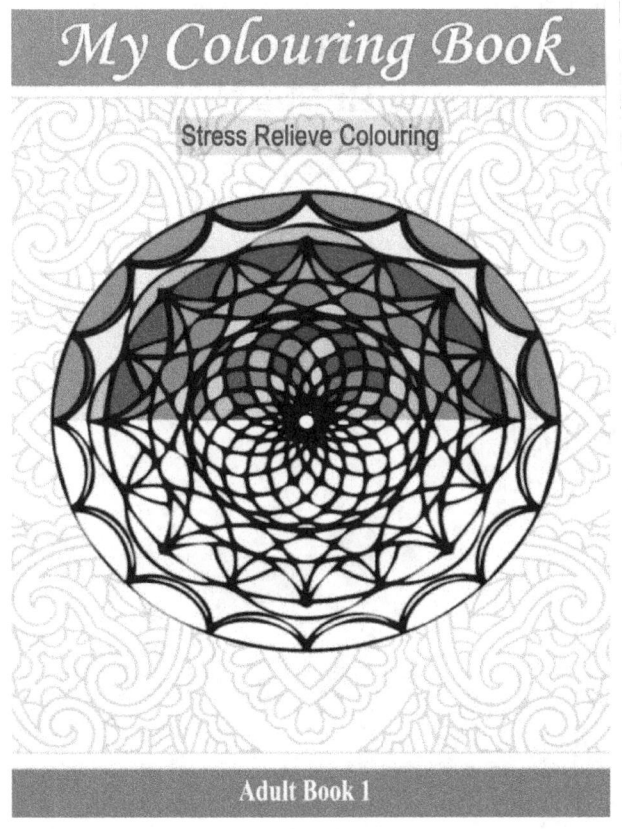

I0390588

Adult Book 1

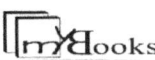

Contents

Tips And Effective Colouring Techniques

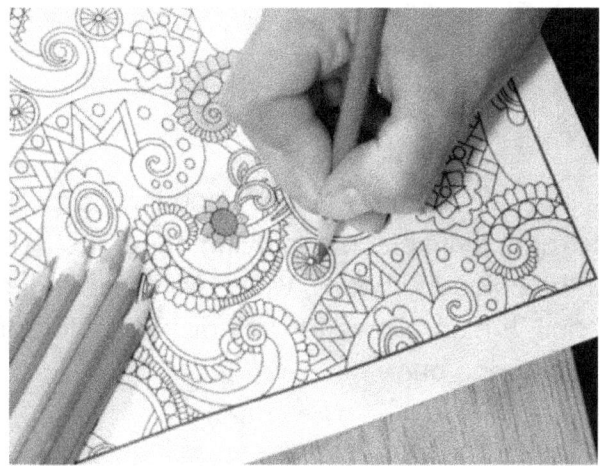

Introduction

Welcome to Colouring Book 1. Adult colouring books have taken off big time, leading to a huge following today. In fact, it's become so popular that this phenomenon looks to be set to stay for some time to come.

The reason for the colouring book phenomenal growing popularity is simple to understand, apart from taking you back to your childhood, and despite any colouring techniques you may be using, colouring 'Mandalas or Patterns', is very therapeutic, and addictive. There are some experts that take it even further, indicating that involving yourself in the colouring process is as relaxing as doing meditation or yoga, giving the colourer the same beneficial results.

Colouring engages your imagination and creativity, and this is where your colouring practice comes into play. Below, I have included five different colouring techniques to help improve your skills. I have included as much information as possible with each technique, enough information to at least get you started.

So let's get you started...

There are several options when it comes to colouring tools, and they include:

- crayons
- coloured pencils
- gel pens
- fine-tip markers

A good technique I use all the time when colouring, is to use my freshly sharpened coloured pencils, etc, on a plain piece of playing paper first. This will take the sharpness away from the tip of the colouring pencil, which will leave a deeper colour when you first begin to use the pencil. It also allows for any disintegration of the tip, which can leave quite a mess on the colouring page.

And in this way, if things don't work out like you planned, your pages won't be won't be ruined.

It's important to understand, that not every method works well with every technique, something you should always keep in mind before you start your colouring. For example, markers work very well with some methods, whereas, crayons and coloured pencils may work better with others.

I found the best way to find the best colouring method was to experiment and have fun along the way, this in itself can bring great satisfaction and pleasure.

Blending Techniques

Believe it or not, but there are several things you can use to help you blend colours, most are inexpensive and close to hand.

Here are just a few of them:

- **Water**... Freely available, works great when using 'Watercolour' pencils. After you have finished colouring your page, simply wet a paintbrush and 'repaint' the areas you want to blend.
- **Eraser** or rubber... Is a great at blending colours too? How can something that removes pencil be any good at blending colours... it just works,

don't use too much pressure, start by lightly rubbing the area gently. A large eraser works best in larger areas. Use a pencil eraser for smaller areas.

- **Nail polish remover**... 'Yes' you read that right, it's another excellent blending medium, and it's the number one choice for some colouring experts too. To use this method, simply pour a little bit of the remover into a cap, then dipping your brush into it, brush over the areas you want to blend. Tip; if you are using coloured pencils, this is a great way to remove any grooves.
- Using a **White pencil**... I used this method all the time with great success. Start by lightly rubbing the white pencil over the area you wish to blend, increasing intensity if required.
- A **blending marker** is another idea. It works like the blending pencil, mentioned above, by dissolving and blending the colour right on the paper. It's a good idea to use these markers in a ventilated room, because the vapours leave a pretty strong smell.
- If you're working with **Crayons**... For this method you will require a Q-tip and some mineral oil. Simply dunk the swab into the oil and lightly rub it over the colours you want to blend... That's it.

Shading Techniques

Most shading techniques generally tend to work better when using coloured pencils. One of the most successful ways to practice is to use two contrasting colours. Use the first colour to shade from left to right. Use the second colour to shade in the opposite direction.

Now practice blending these two colours together, meeting in the middle.

Believe it or not, but the way in, which you hold the pencil, can make a big difference to your outcome. I know this may sound obvious, but try positioning the pencil so that most of its tip is in contact with the paper. This will make the colour process a whole lot smoother, and can help to dramatically reduce the possibility of any pencil lines... this is better accomplished by holding the pencil somewhat sideways.

Another tip; most people tend to use white and black to do their shadowing, but it's a lot better to use colours like dark blue and purple instead... Give it a go you may be surprisingly delighted with the results. Tip; try using light yellows, for the highlights, again you will be surprised at the outcome.

Whatever you do, **DON'T** ever be tempted to rub colours together to create the shadings you desire, experience has shown that this method tends to smear everything together, it doesn't work very well and you may end up ruining your colouring efforts.

Doodling Drawing Your Own Image

It's surprising just how many people doodle when concentrating, or listening to an intense conversation. Believe it or not, but this is the natural artist in you, and we all have some artistic talent. You can learn to develop this talent, turning it into a very good way to make an income. This usually happens, because you're in an artistic mood, and when there's no colouring book insight, and this is why we tend to doodle.

Next time you find yourself doodling, just try to stay in the mood and expand on the image you are drawing, you may be pleasantly surprised at the outcome, but remember these are unique drawings and if extensive you could turn them into colouring images.

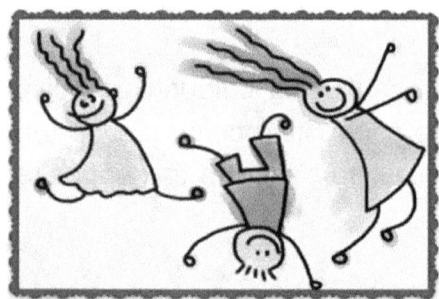
Doodling does not have to be confined to just using a pencil, as your skills increase then start to use, for example, pastels, chalk, and paints. When people doodle they aren't necessarily aware of the amount of concentration been applied when doodling, it has the same beneficial effects as colouring in images in a colouring book.

Some experts claim to be able to tell your moods, and personal problems when examining your doodling efforts. For example, a simple round face may indicate you are a happy person, and a menacing expression may point to someone who is somewhat unsociable.

Having said that when you draw of faces why not draw them with different expressions, this way you learn how to end up with a more realistic looking face. Then take it further by introducing more features to the same face, going on to drawing an entire page of noses, eyes, ears, etc, remembering that practice makes perfect.

You could then go on to drawing family members, friends, and then everyday objects. Even try injecting a little humour, or silliness into your drawings.

Doodling, as a beneficial pastime, which is probably much more popular than you realise. Famous presidents, authors and celebrities, all admit to doing some doodling on a regular basis. The more you relax and let your hands do most of the work; you're well on your way to being a 'master doodler'.

You never know where this may end, you could go on to become an established artist in your own rights, why not give it a try?

Using Gel Pen Techniques with Shading

Lots of adult colouring enthusiasts LOVE to use get pens, which can be used to pull off several fun techniques and pretty respectable shadings too. One of the biggest benefits of using this type of pen is its ability to keep its shape and size, unlike crayons or coloured pencil, which alter the more you use them.

Hatching

Hatching is easy-peasy and the concept is simple to understand. It consists of a bunch of parallel lines or strokes, which results in a uniformed look. You can use multiple colours and angle the lines any direction you like. Crisscrossing the lines makes for an even more interesting look.

Stippling

In a nutshell 'Stippling' are drawings that use 'Dots' to construct the image, the more dots you use the darker the texture of the image becomes. Stippling is rarely used on its own, but is quite often combined with 'Hatching', (see above).

Shading

The shading techniques described in this book, work quite well with a gel pen, although it does take lots of practice to achieve your goals. A blending pen typically consists of two tips filled with a clear fluid and when you draw over a colour with the pen, the clear fluid helps the colours blend together.

When you have finished with the pen, remember to scribble with the pen on a spare piece of paper until the pen runs dry of the fluid.

Most enthusiasts recommend only using the gel pens near to the outline of the drawing you are colouring in. Then with the blending pen, start drawing from the outline to the centre of the sections you are colouring.

Mixing and Layering

If this is your first attempt at colouring, or indeed, if this is a return to colouring after some time off, then welcome to the club. I recommend that you start by using colour pencils, and also start back at the basics, working your way up to a more proficient level.

One of the first rules you'll learn about mixing and layering is...'Practice', and practice more. It's a simple concept, but one that's being born out time after time, the more you practice, the better you get. I can't stress this enough, because people tend to want to punch way above their weight right at the beginning of their colouring experience.

My second rule is... Require 'Patience'. Like any artist who ever walked this Earth, they had to begin somewhere, and so will you.

My third rule is... Keep your pencils sharp. Make sense, well you will be surprised to learn that people tend to forget this rule and wonder why they are never successful with their colouring endeavours.

Keeping your pencils sharp will help you fill in small areas and get right up to the edge of the lines in your drawing, it's also very important to remember NOT to press too hard with the colouring pencil as this will leave darker lines of colour, or grooves. Your goal is always to build up the layers of colour slowly, in this way you achieve the depth of colour you desire. Also remember it's easier to add layers of colour when you need to, because they cannot be removed after.

Something else for you to consider, and I guess, some refer to this has the secret to successfully layering and blending colours, is using the right texture of paper. Your paper should have a fine texture, as opposed to a smooth surface. It's important to understand that it's the texture that holds the colour and allows you to add multiple layers.

Apart from keeping your pencils sharp and using the right texture of paper, successful layering depends on the colours you choose. It's important to choose complementary colours when blending to create the right shadow, and never use a black pencil, because these will make your shadings look dull and flat.

Complementary colours consist of opposites, shades of violet-blue and yellow, orange-red and cyan, green and magenta, etc; my personal preference is to start out using a light colour.

Most people start with coloured pencils, because they layer so well. Applying between, 3 to 5 different layers, you can create a whole new colour.

Just in case you don't know, coloured pencils are waxy, and if you apply too much pressure your colourings will end up looking shiny, which will prevent you building up your layers. So use even strokes and a light to medium touch when colouring.

Conclusion

Although colouring books aren't new, and now Psychiatrists have been recommending colouring as a way to distress your life, as far back as the 1900's. Colouring books have taken off again in a big way over the last couple of years, and there's no doubt that they are here to stay.

Getting involved with the wonderful, colourful, world of colouring books is stimulating, relaxing, and fulfilling, helping you cope with everyday life, bring lots of happiness and enjoyment to you and your loved ones.

You are not alone, colouring books and the number of people who now enjoy nothing more than to complete a colouring task, is growing... and is set to do so way into the not too distant future.

Adult colouring books are now beginning to pop up all over the place, including high-end department stores and catalogues. Small town artists are making names for themselves, earning some extra cash into the bargain.

This is only the tip of the iceberg, in regard to the wonderful and expanding world of adult colouring. As you can see, it's never really been a **'kids only'** activity... even though many grown-ups secretly disagree.

I hope you enjoy your colouring experience, colouring in the Mandalas in this book...

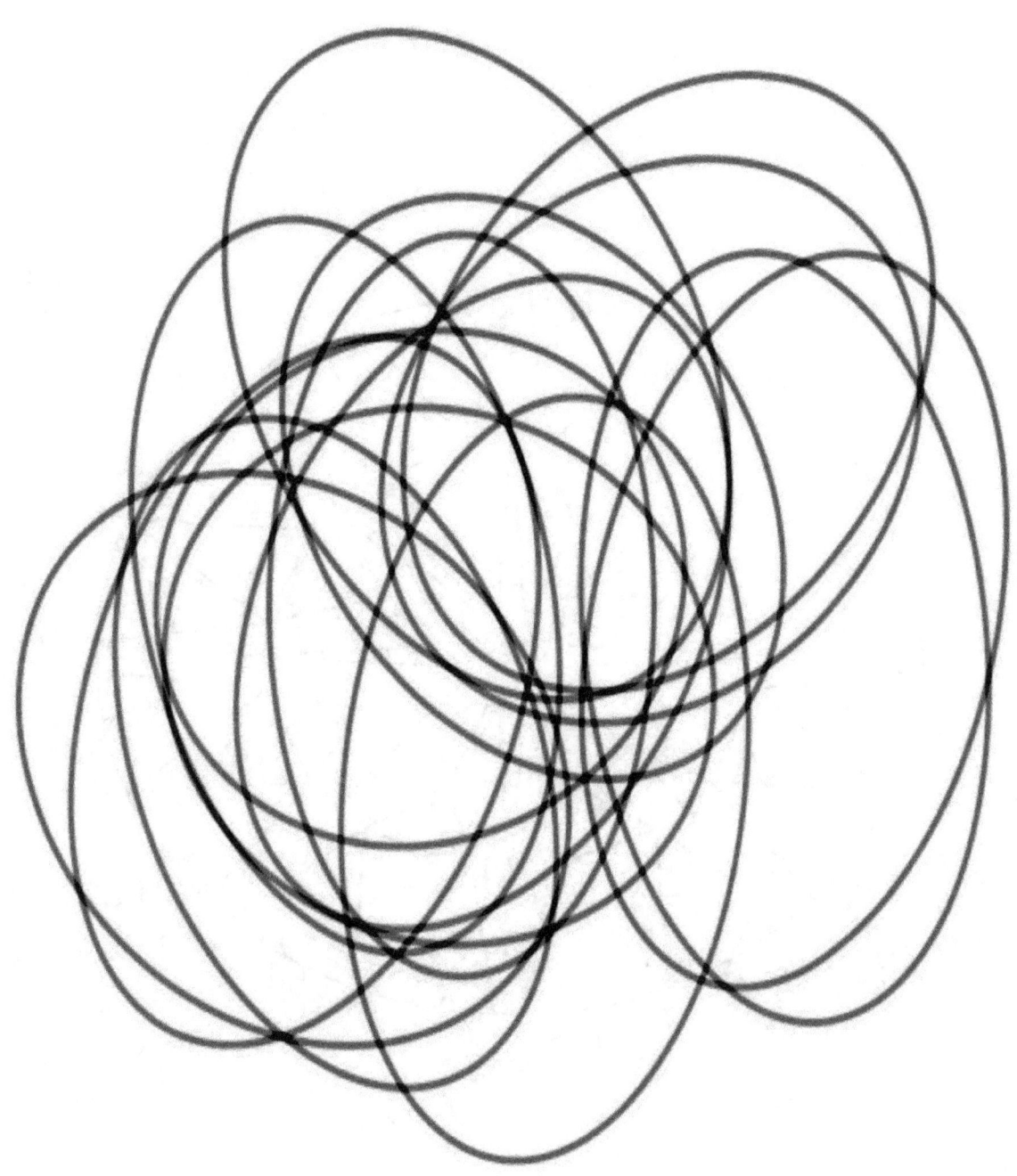

Your Mandalas Enjoy!

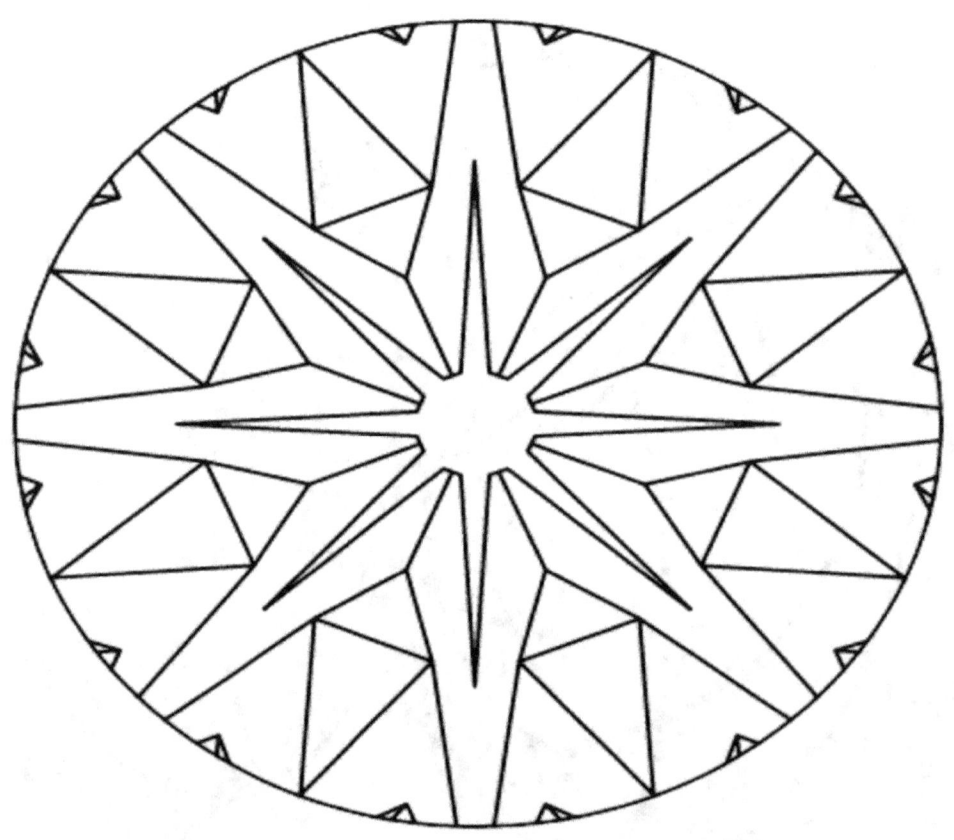

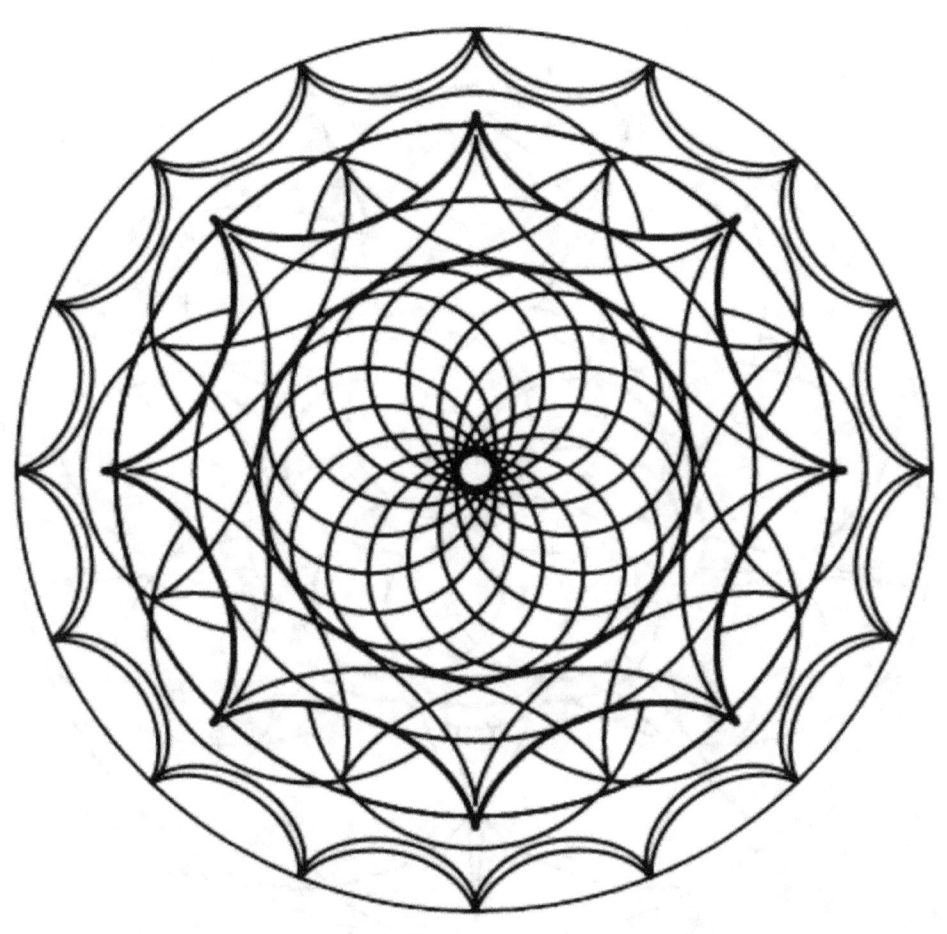

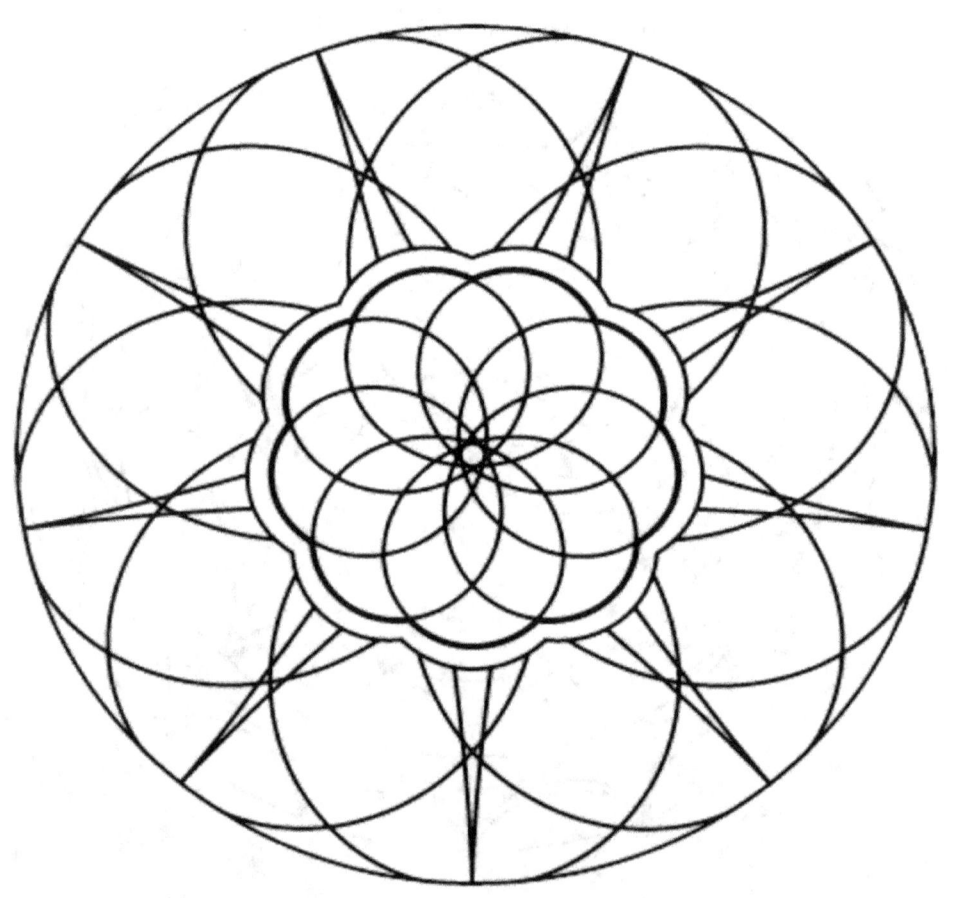

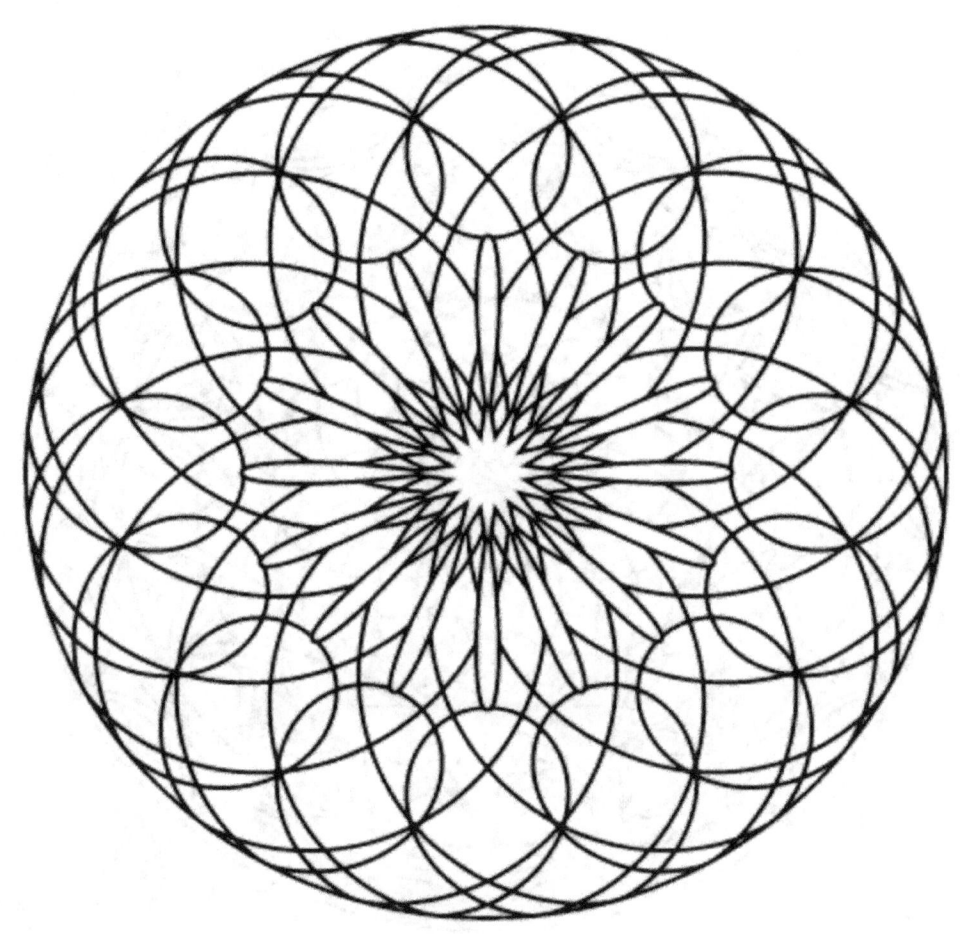

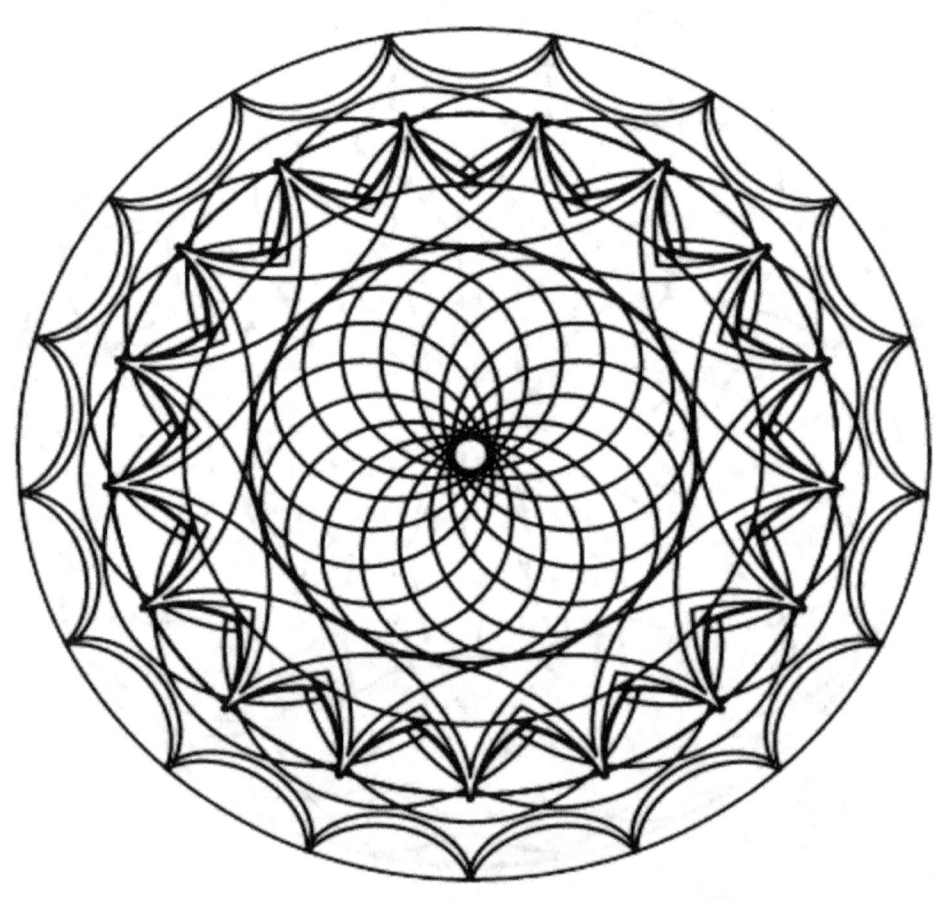

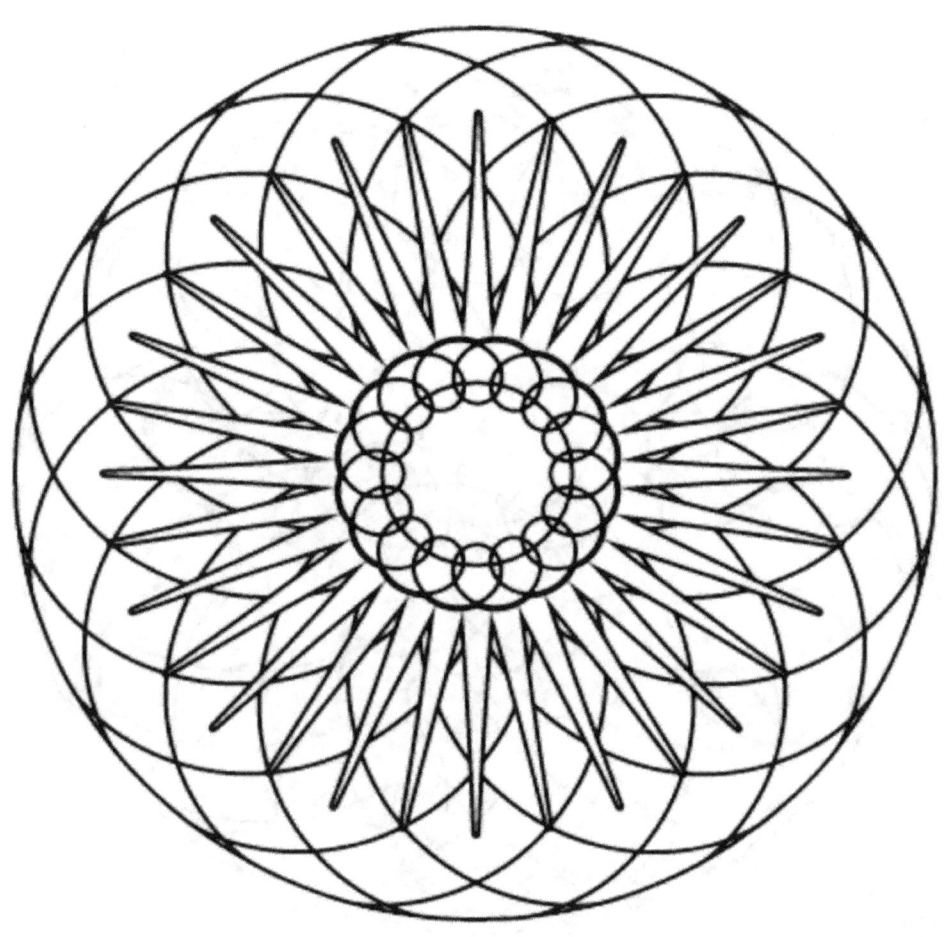

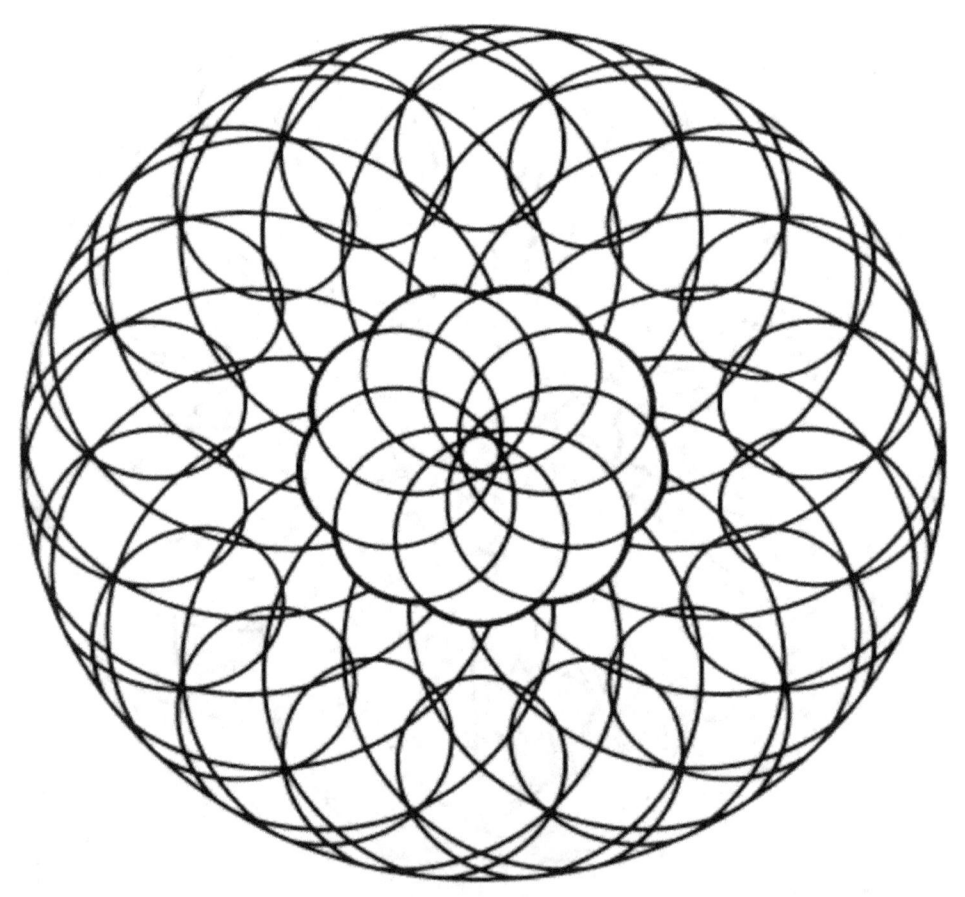

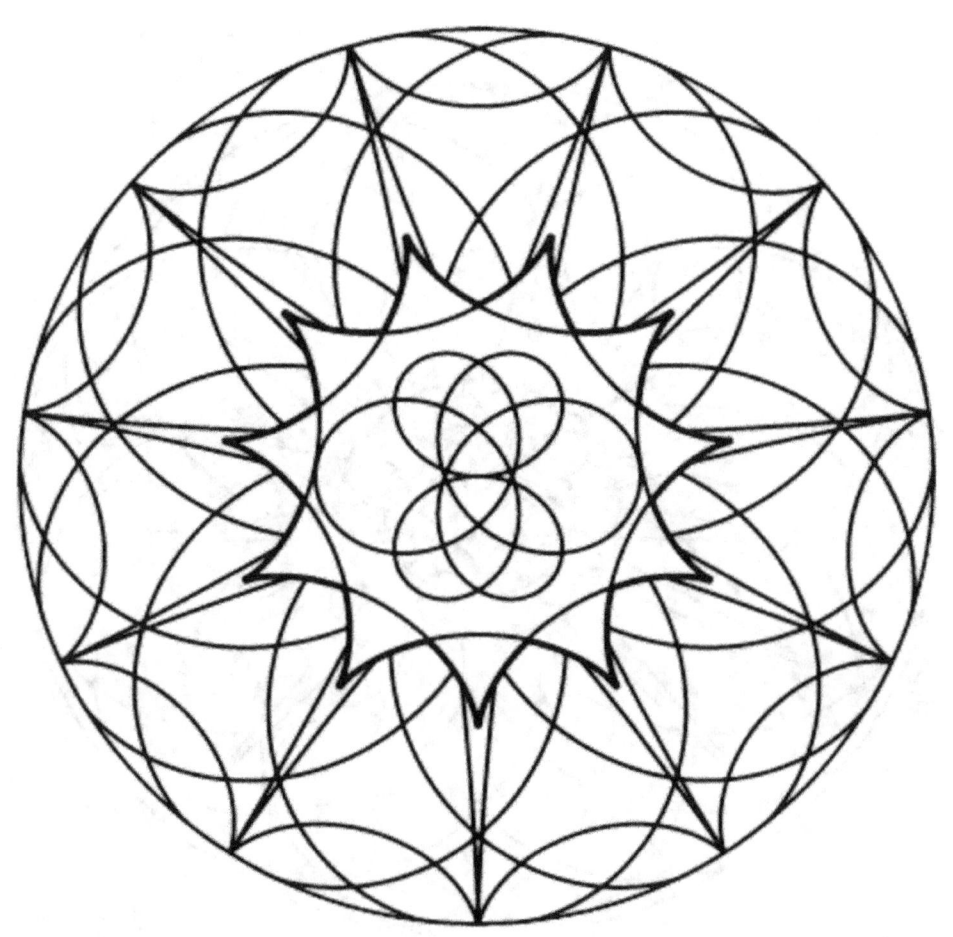

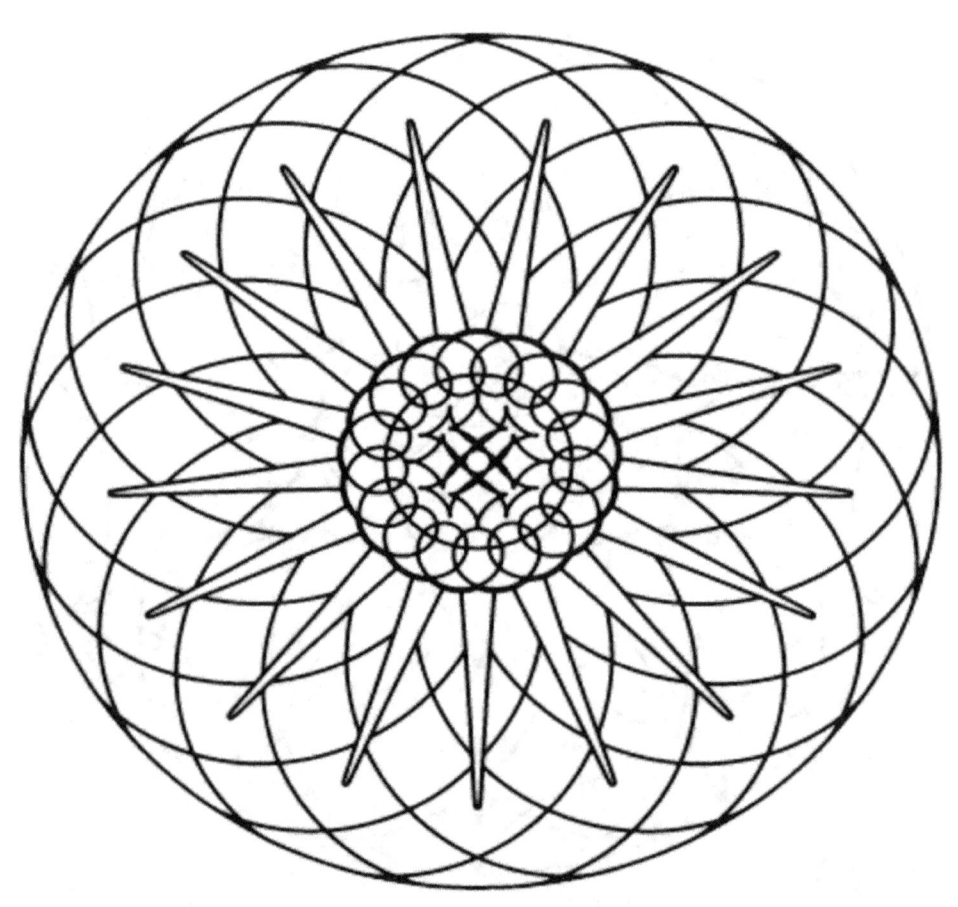

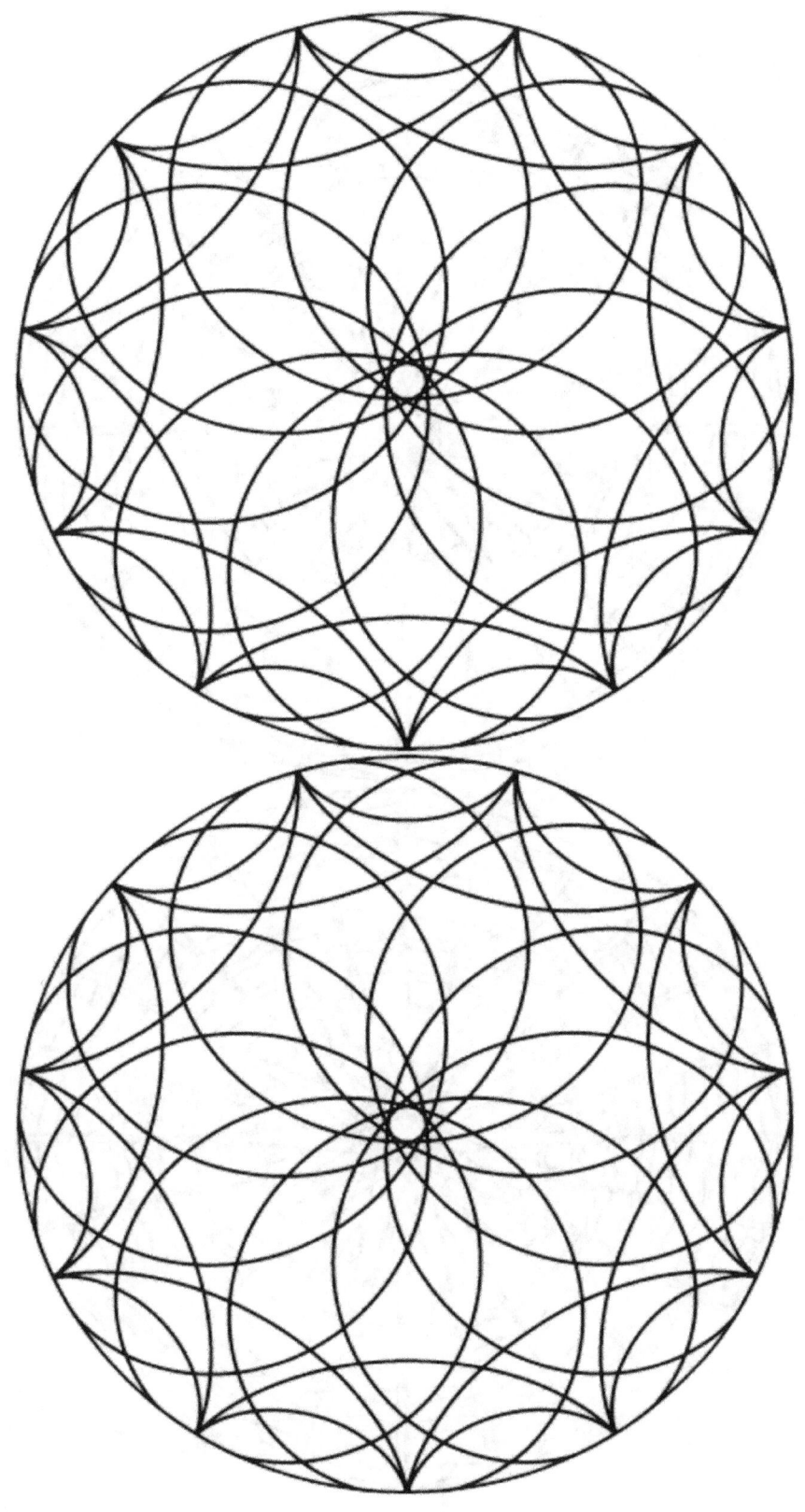

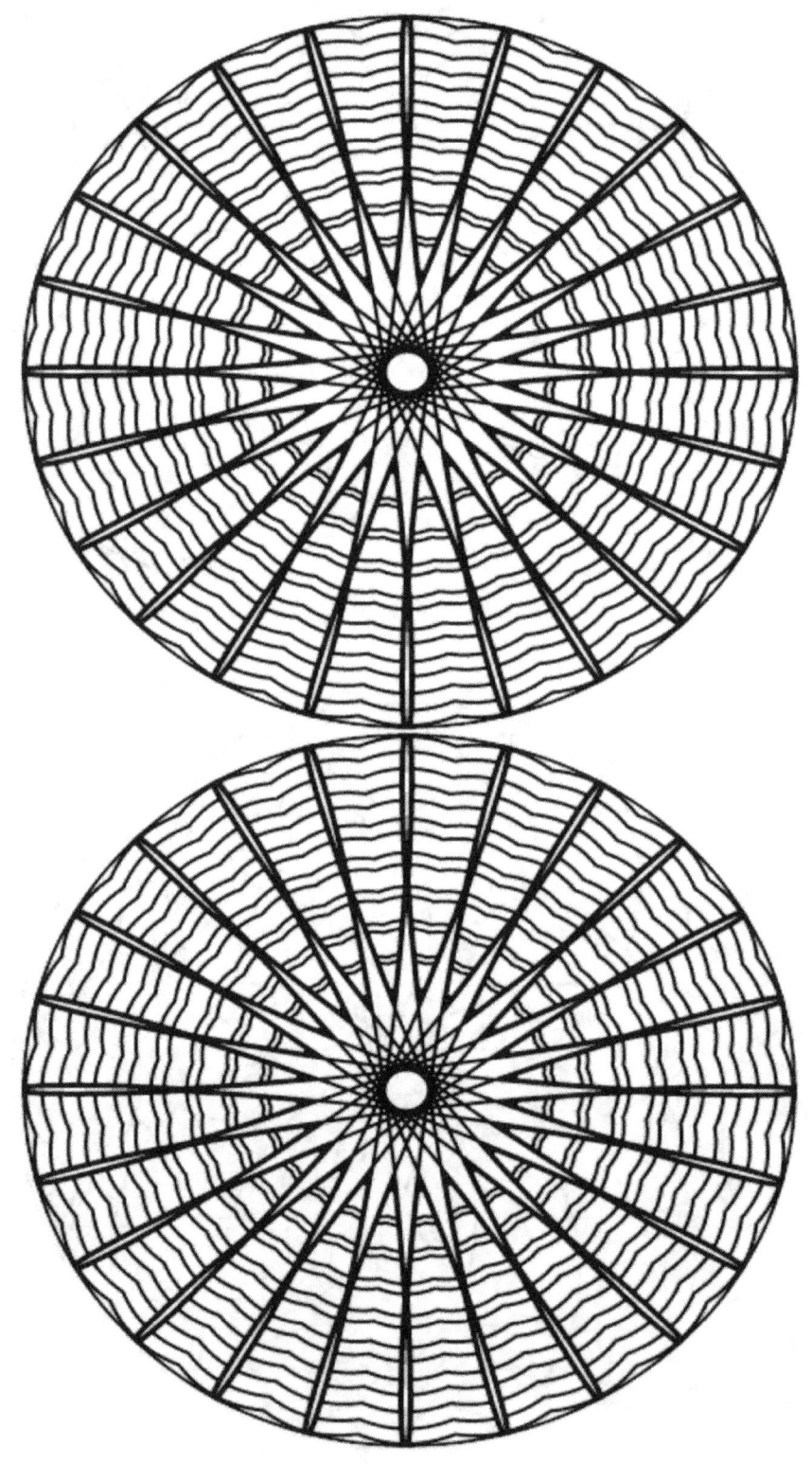

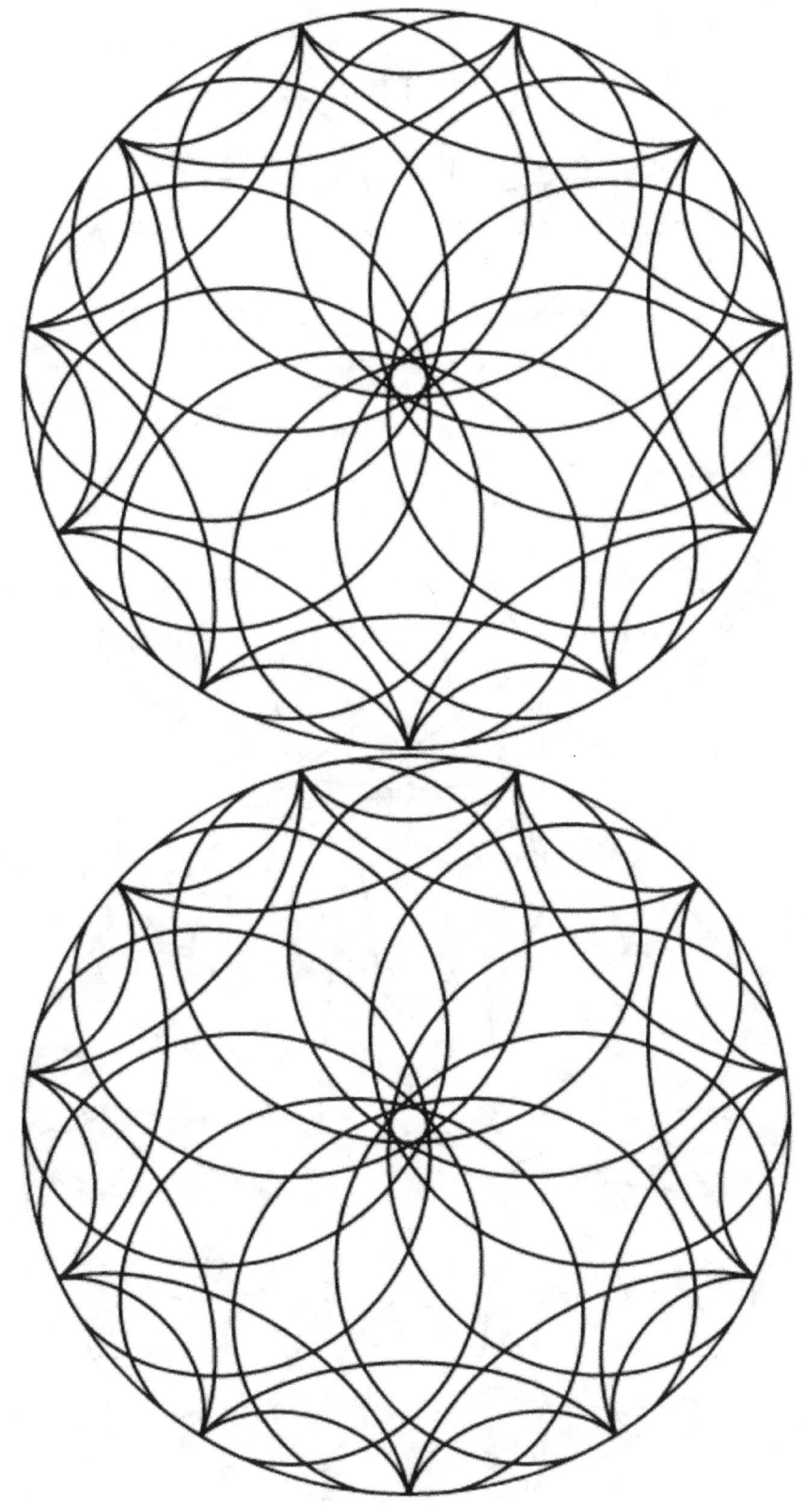

23

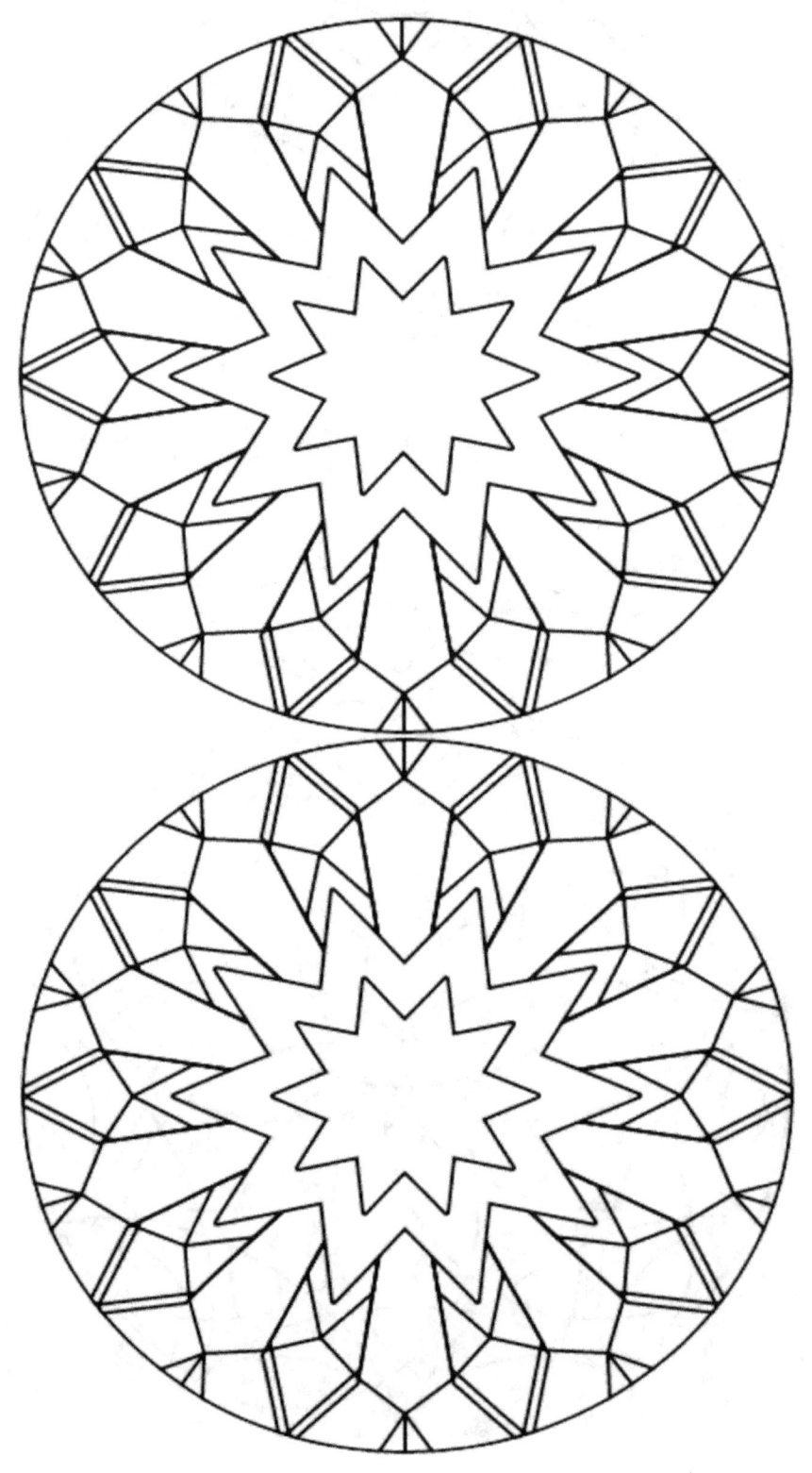

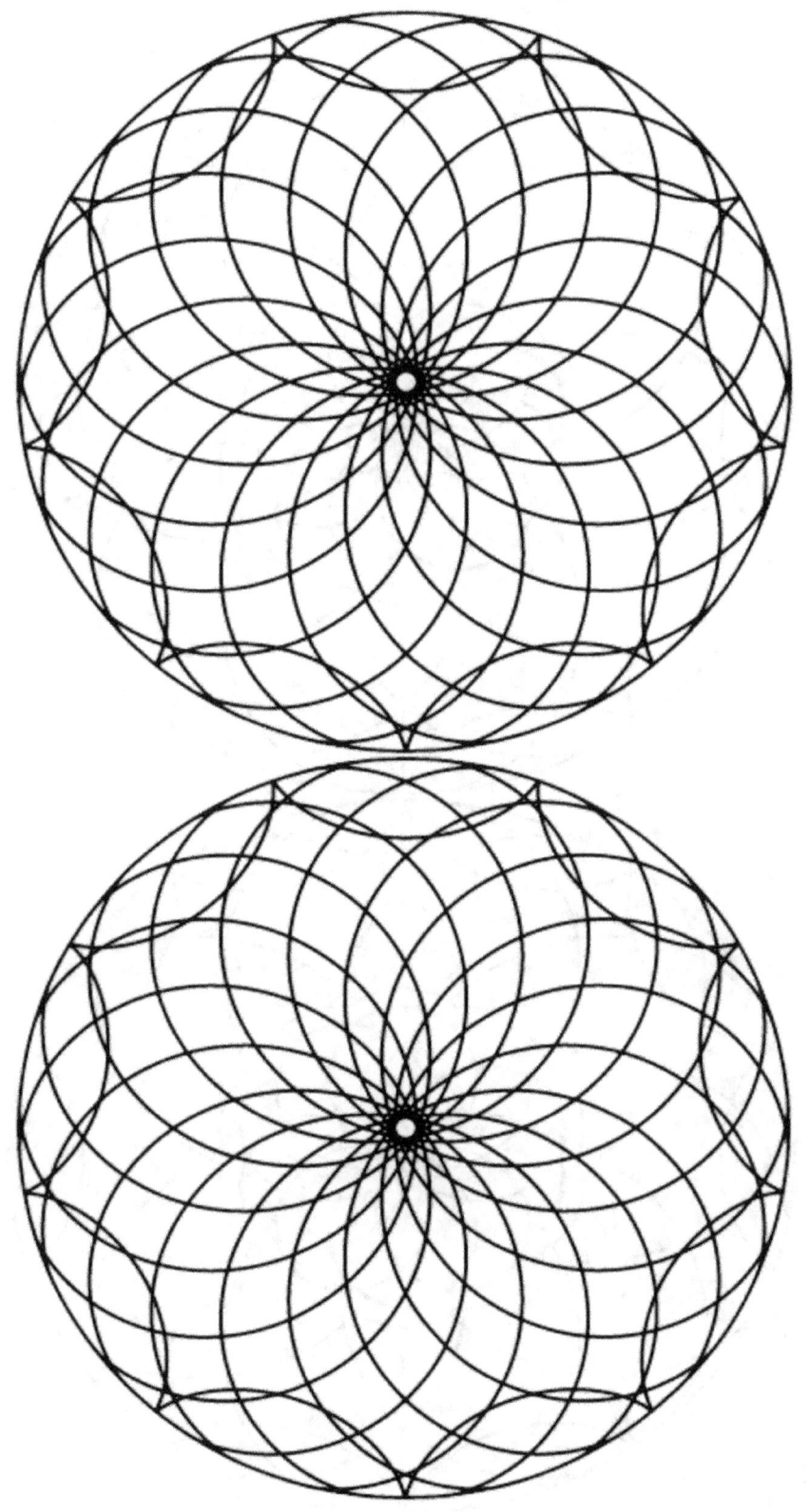

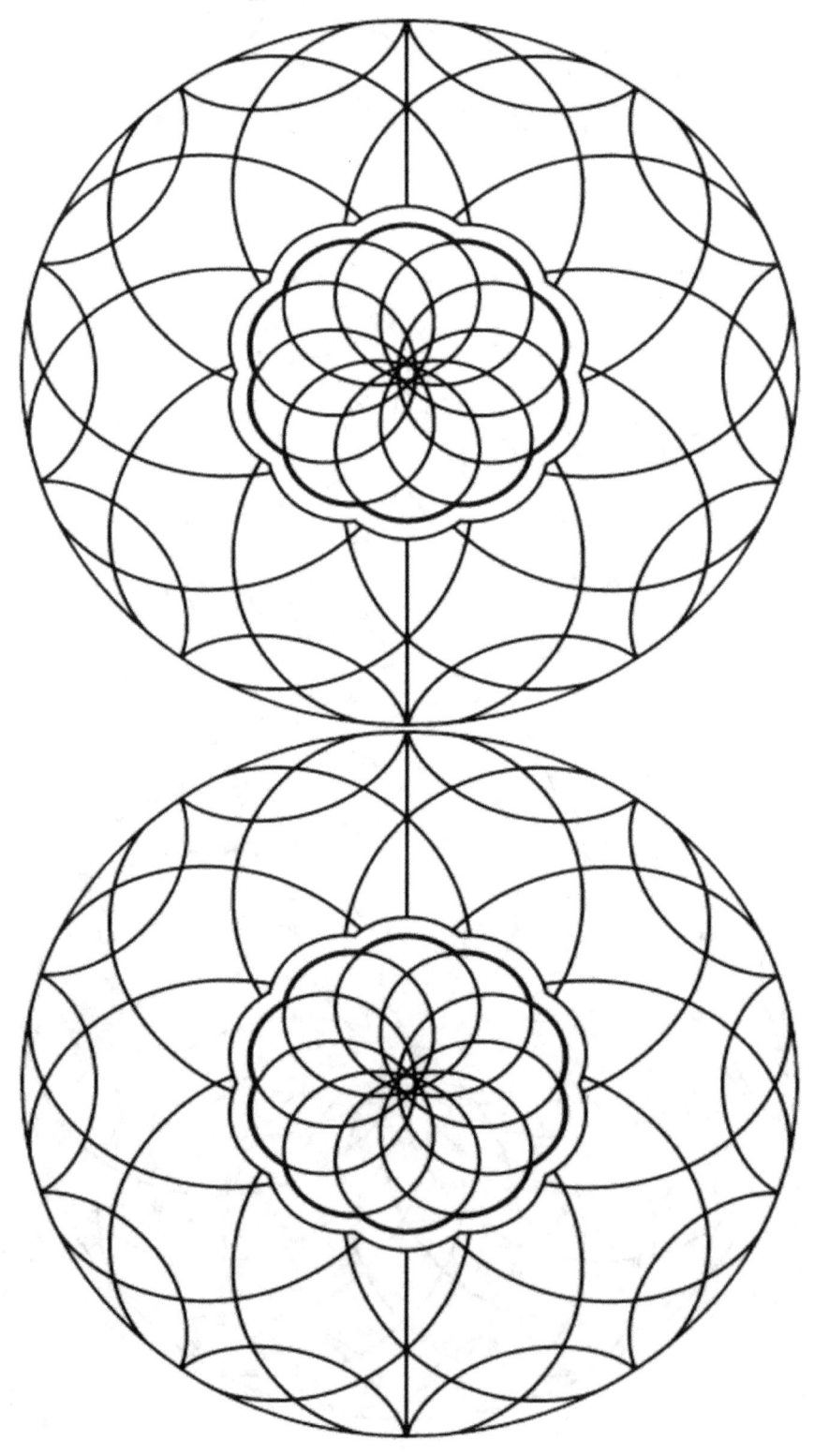

26

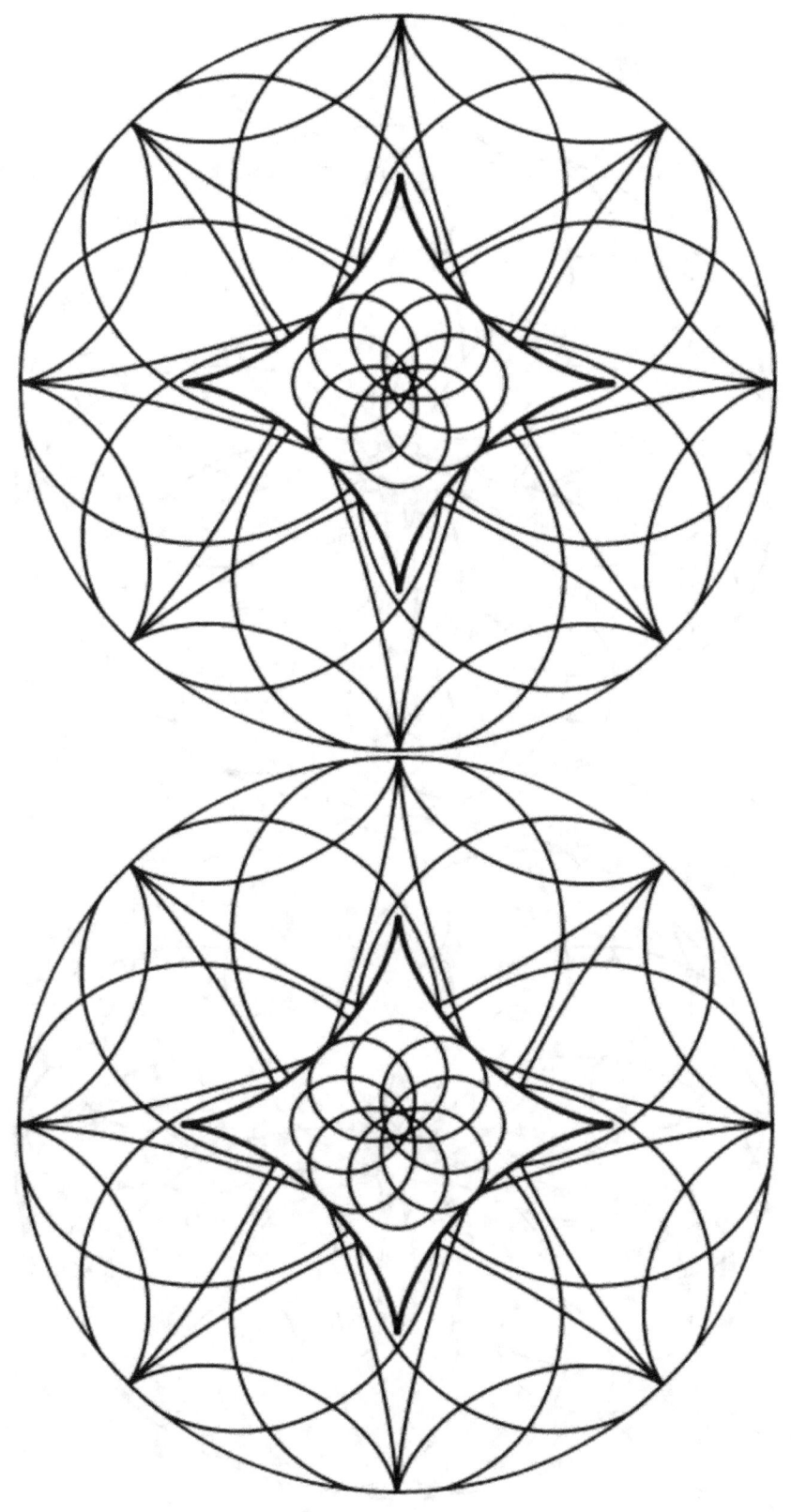

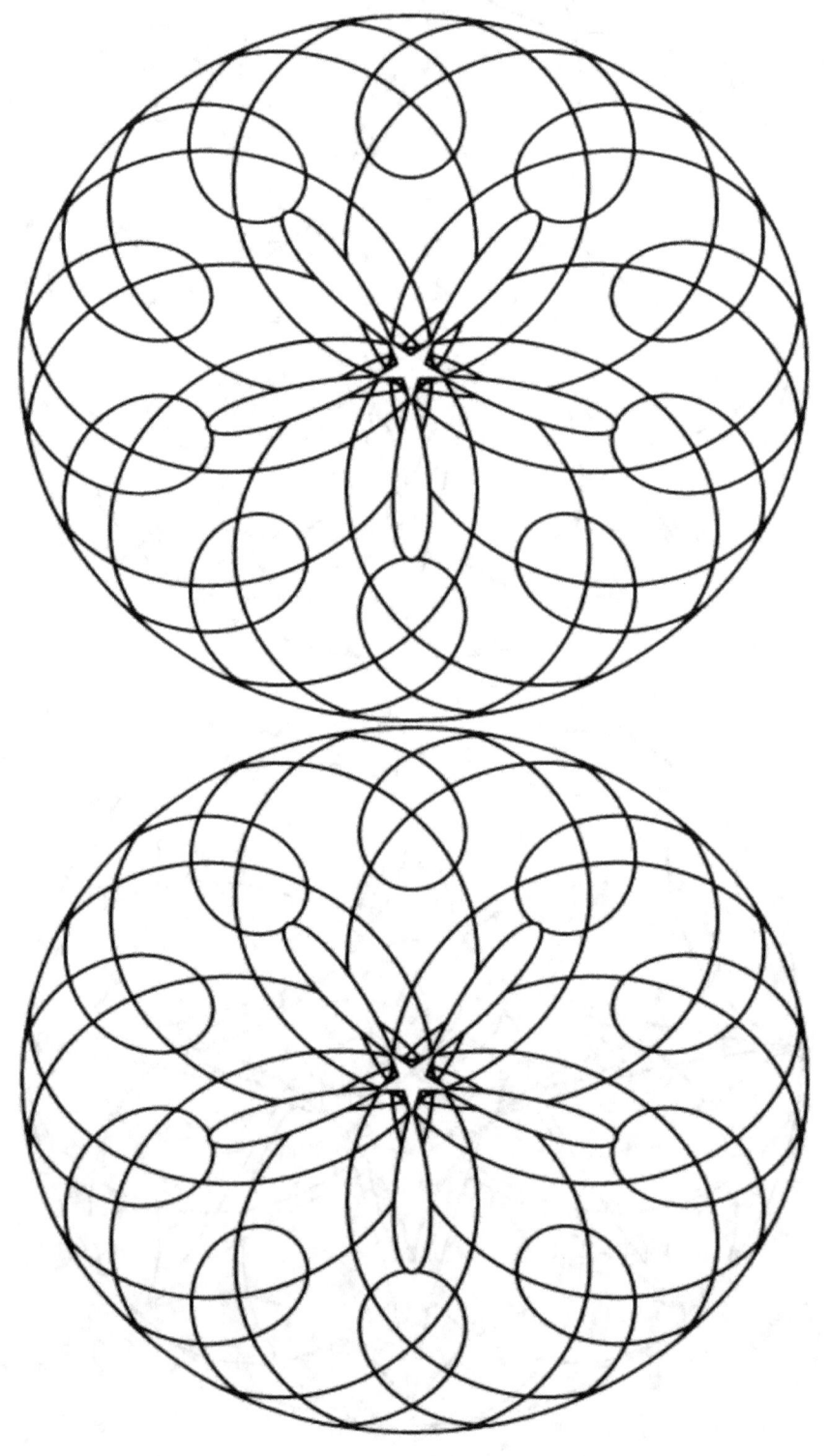

28

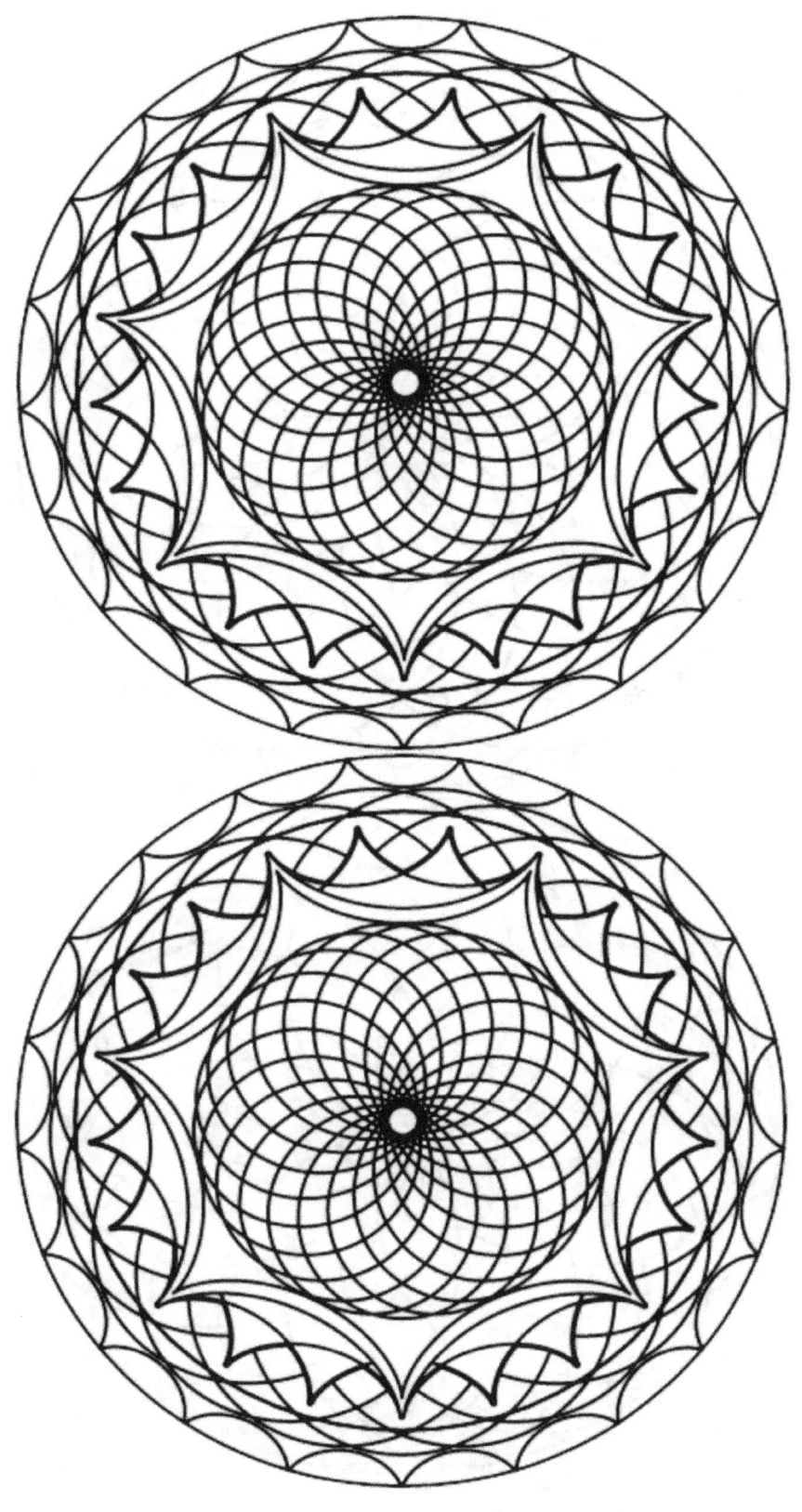

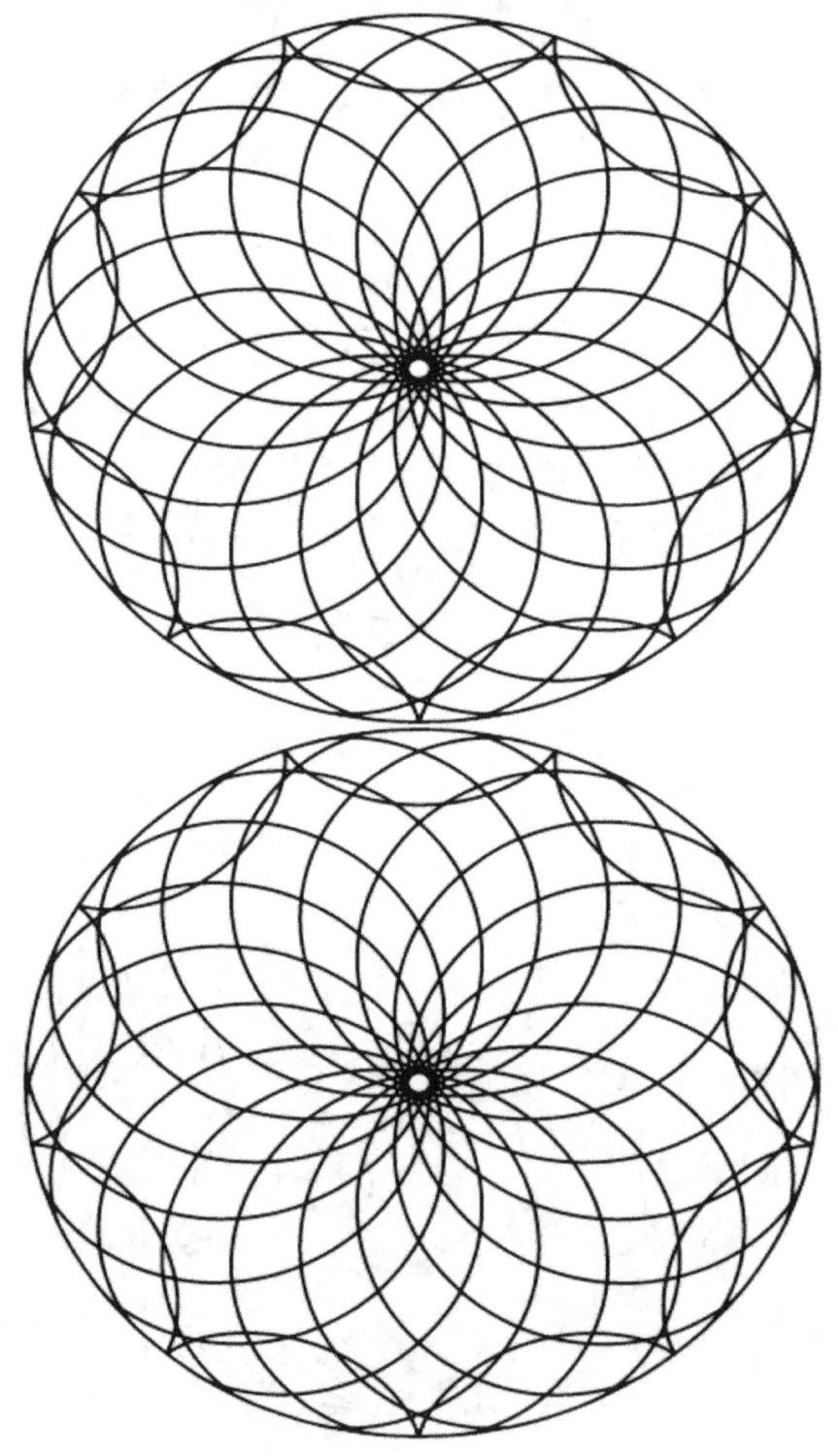

30

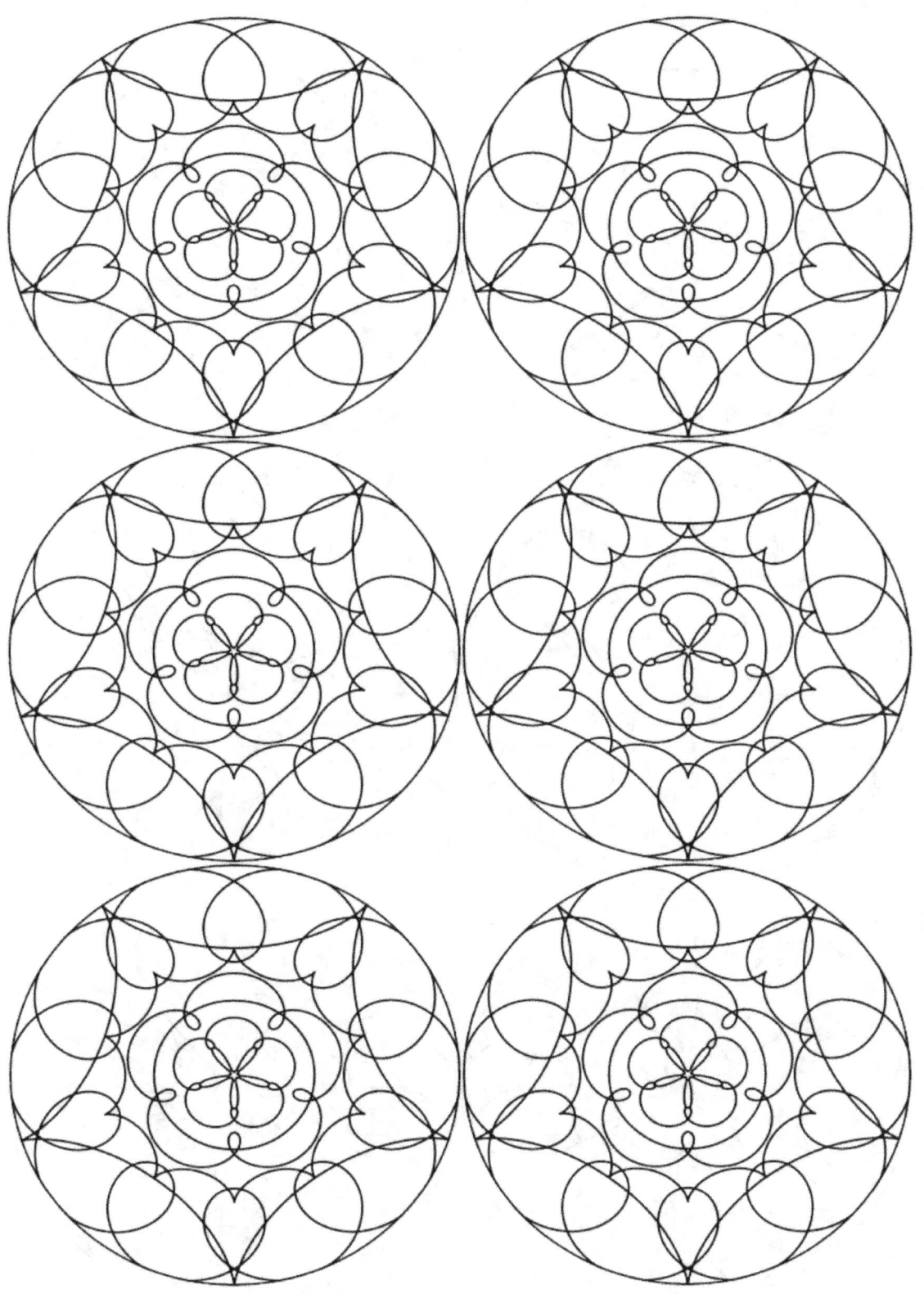

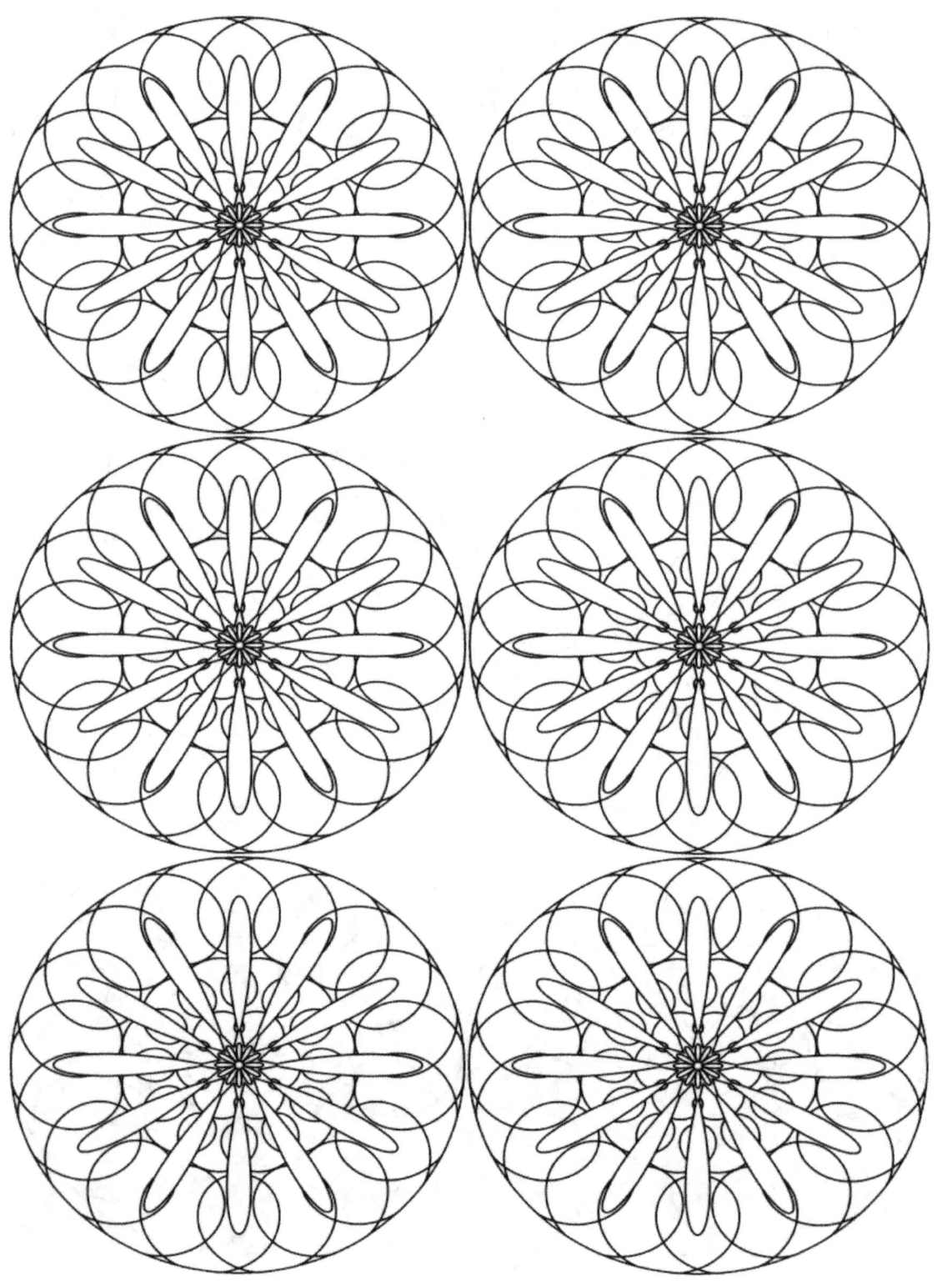

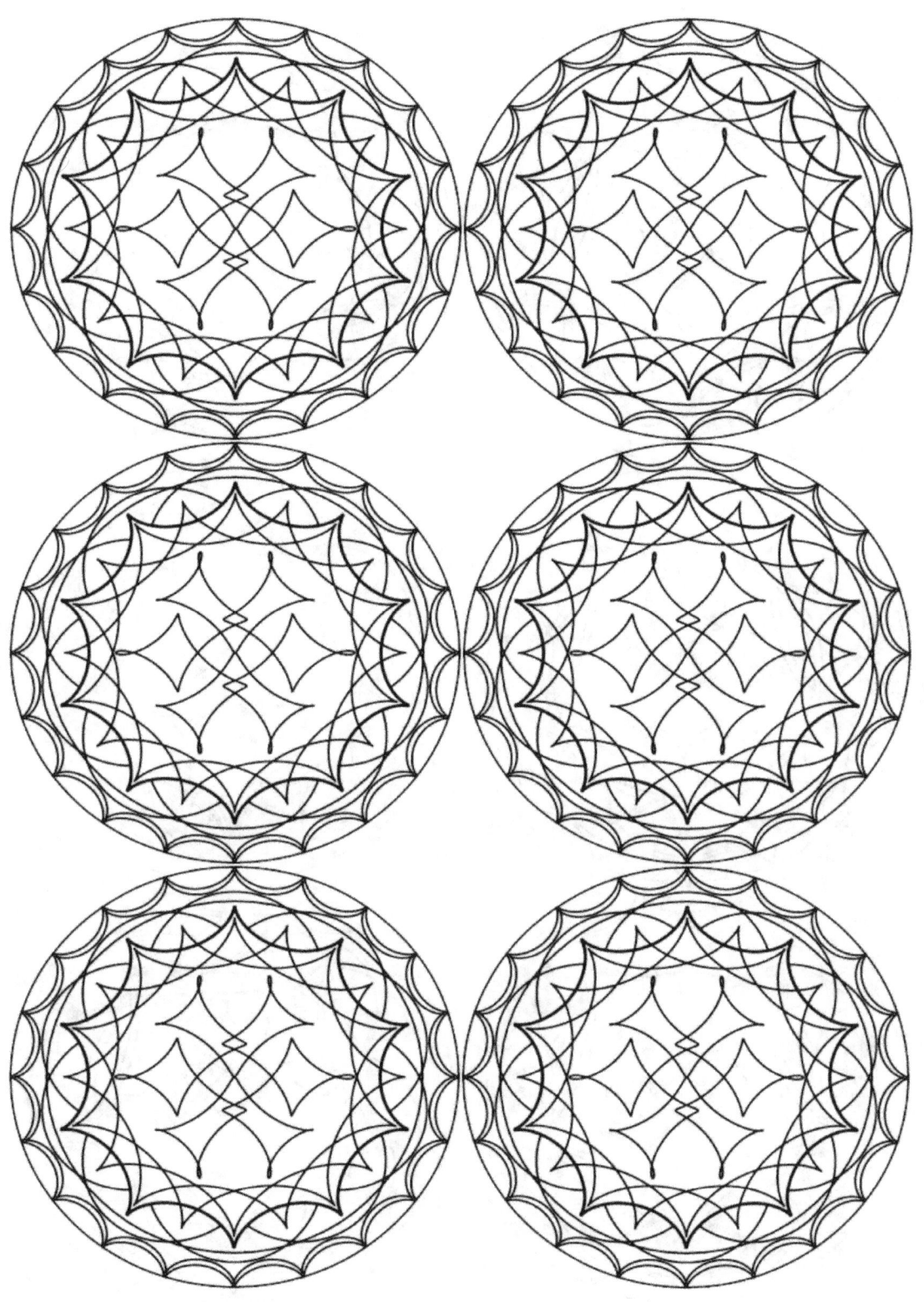

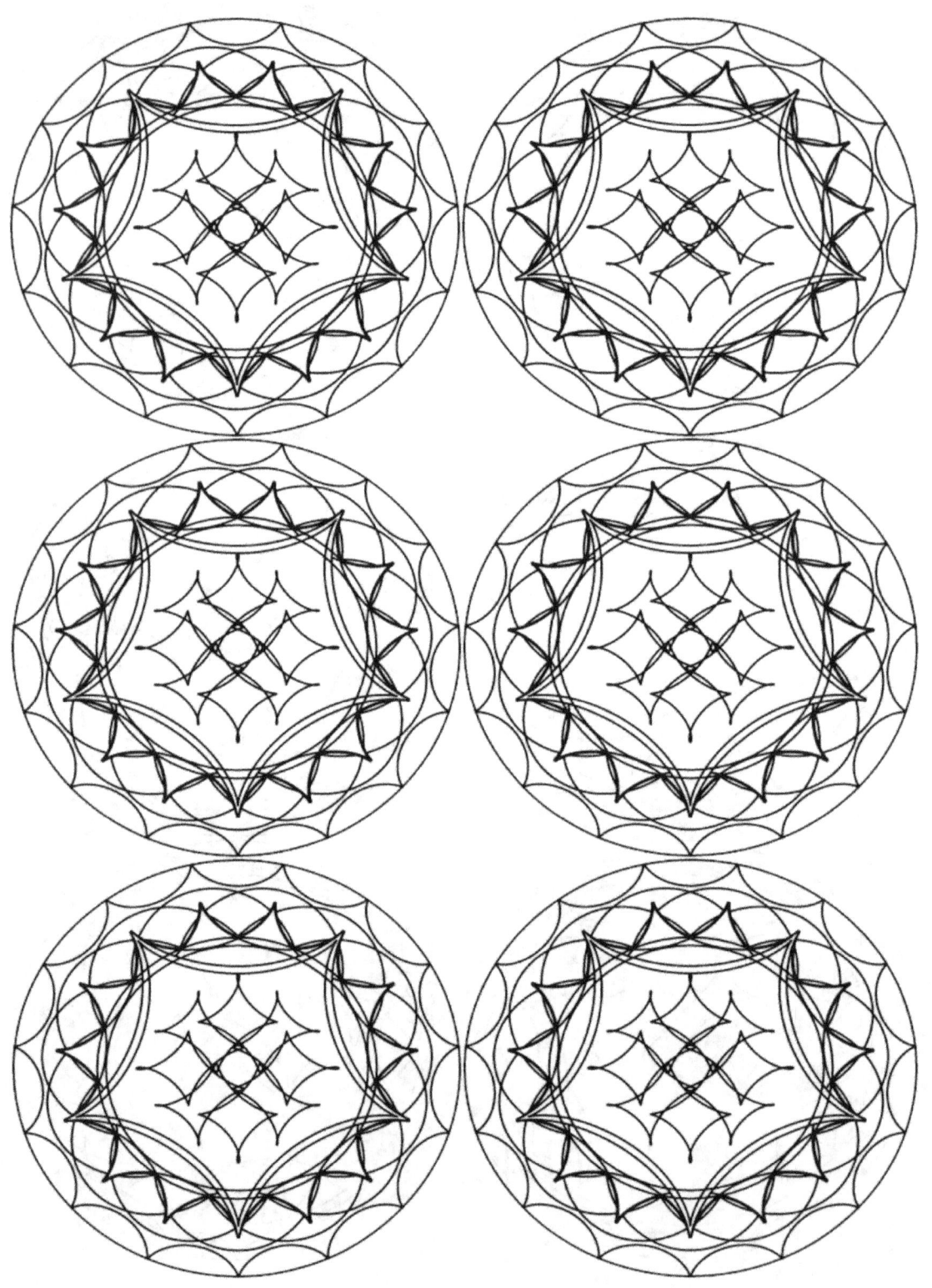

34

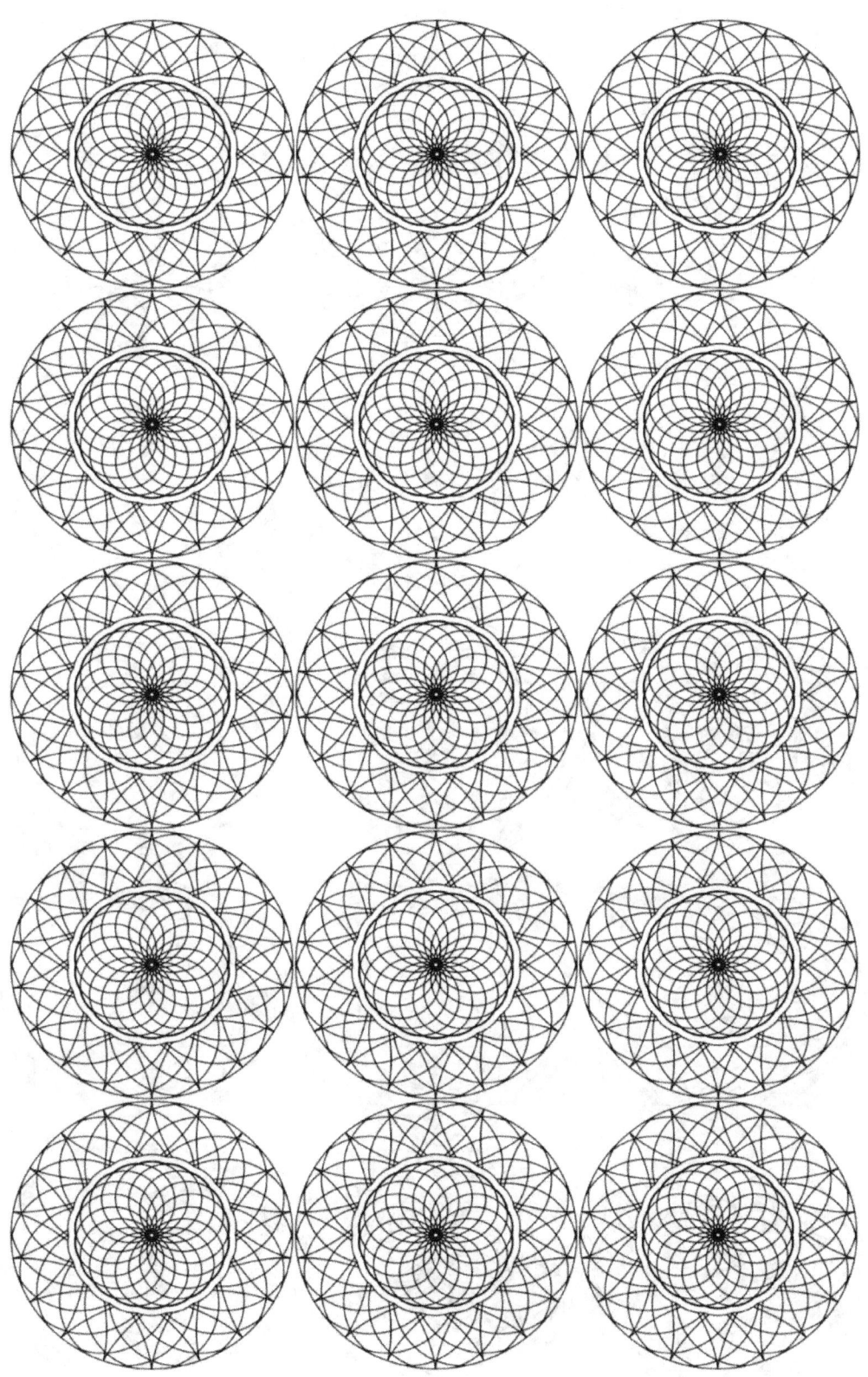

35

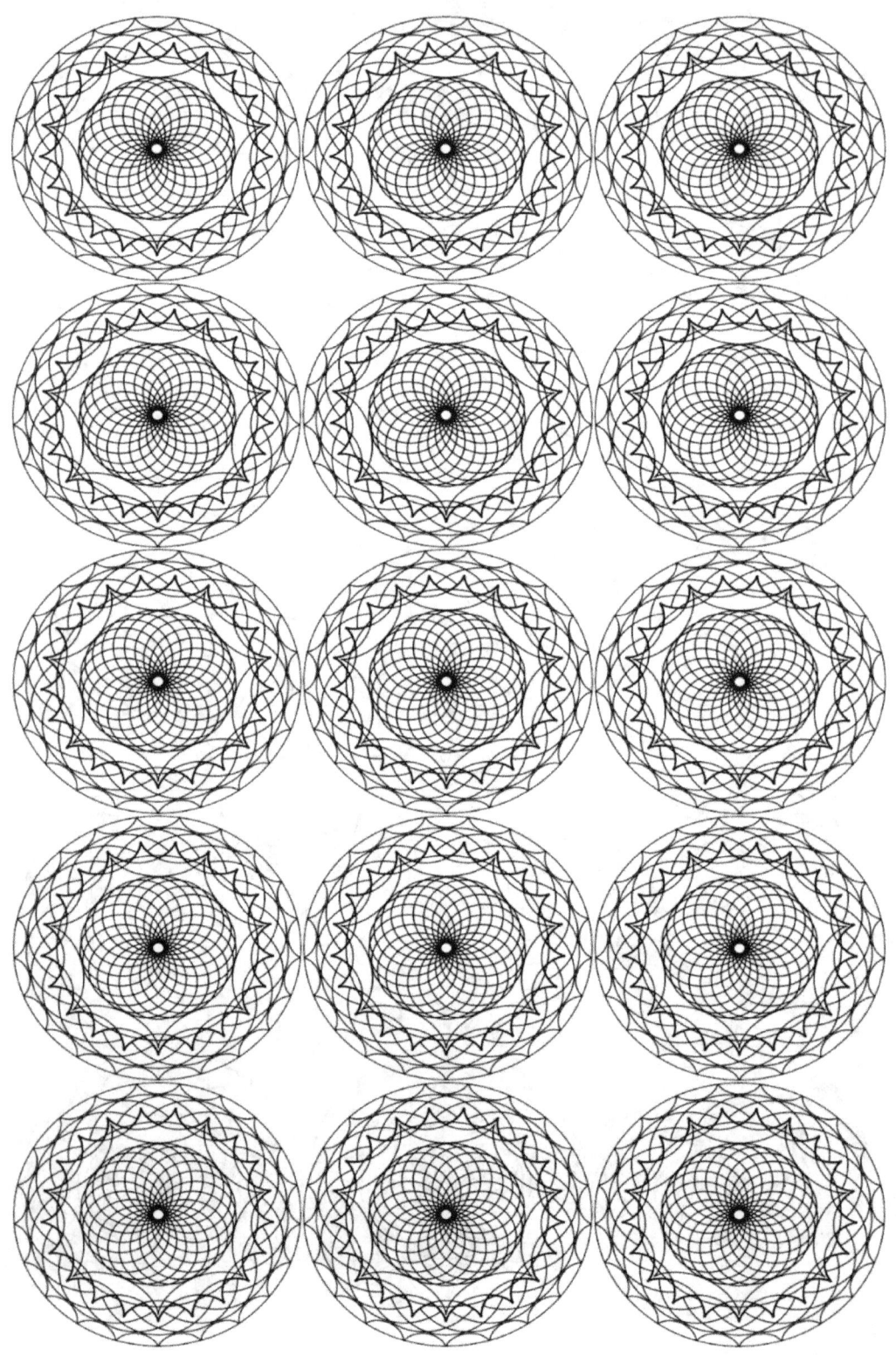

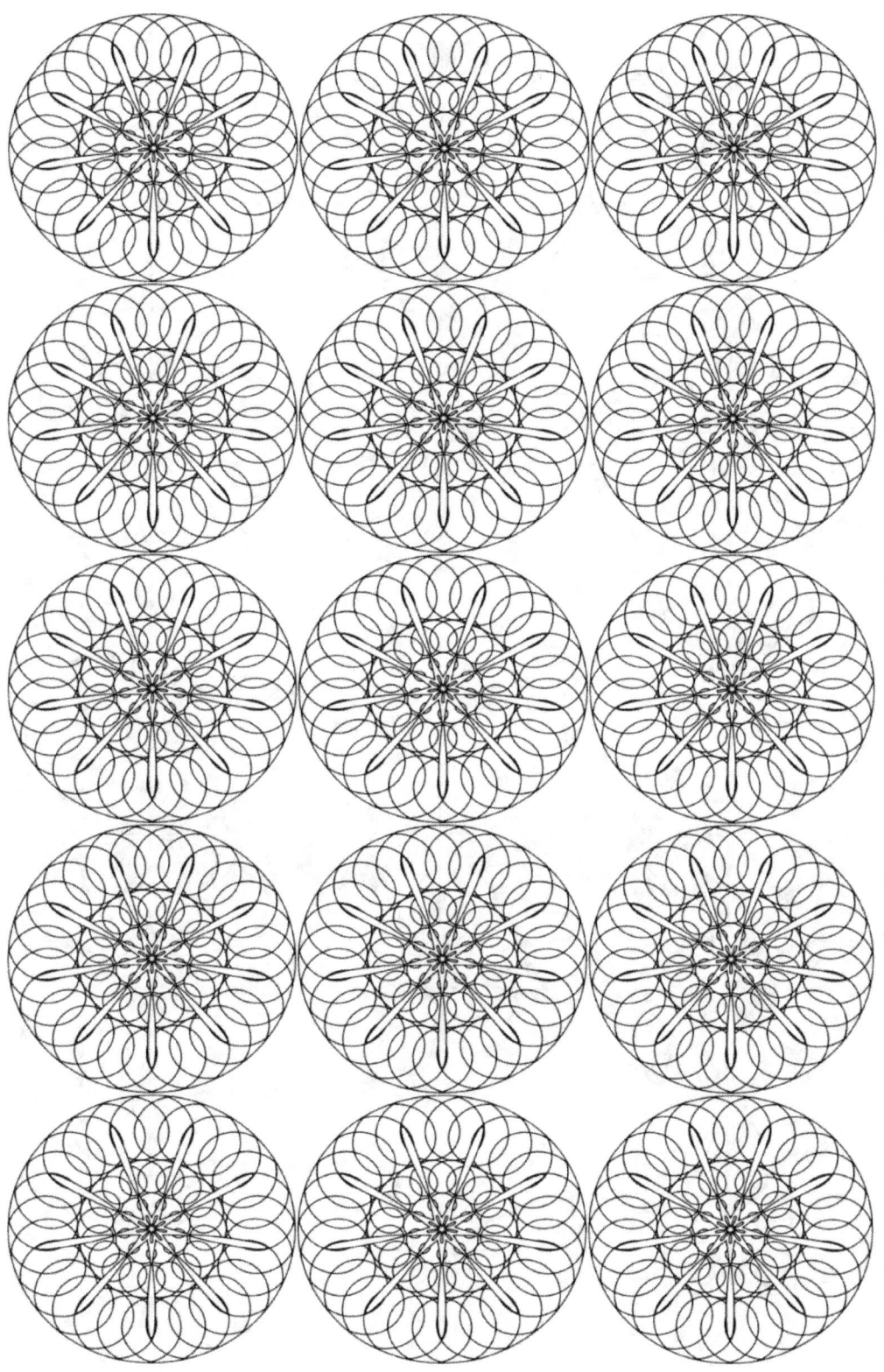

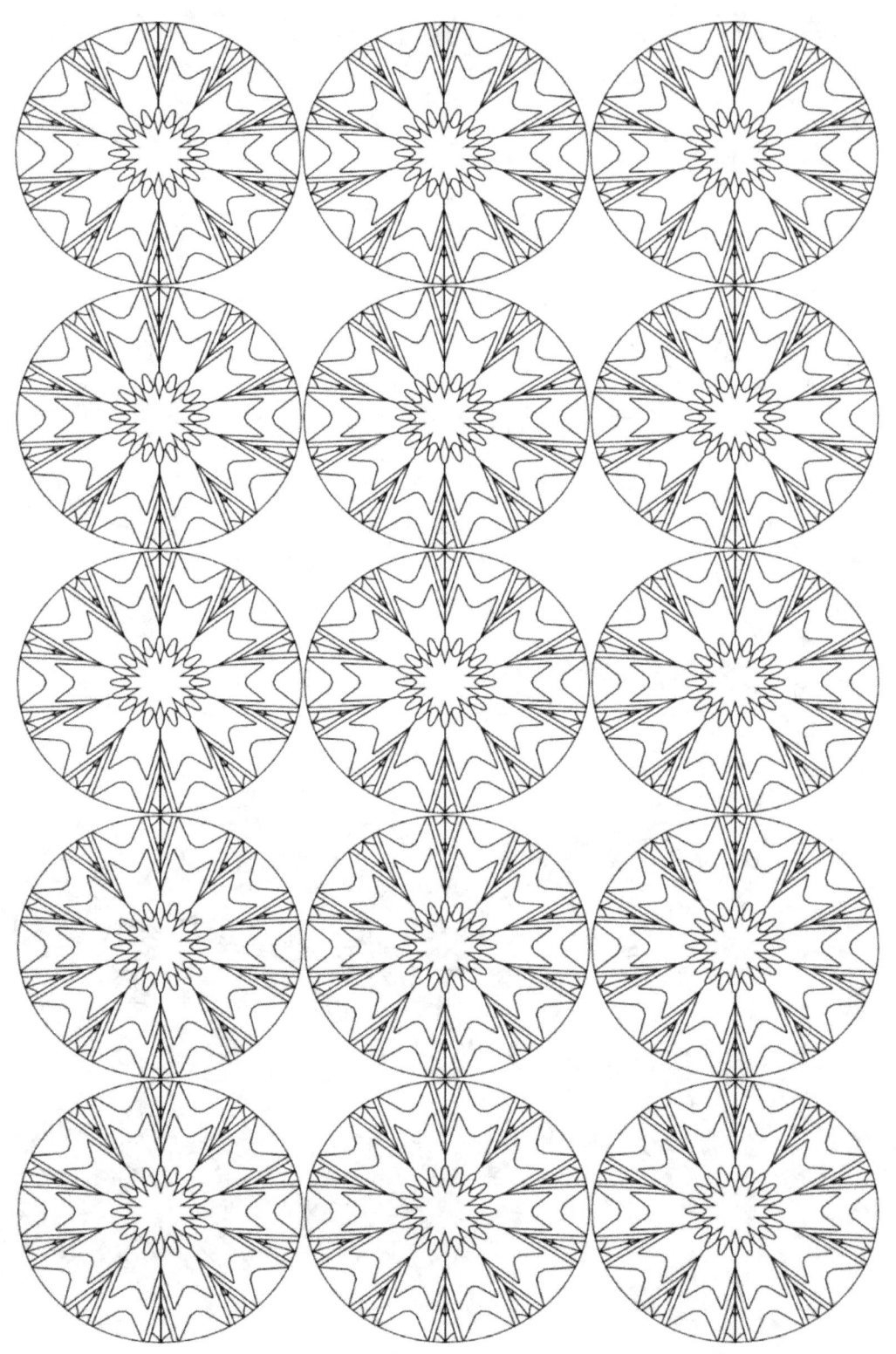

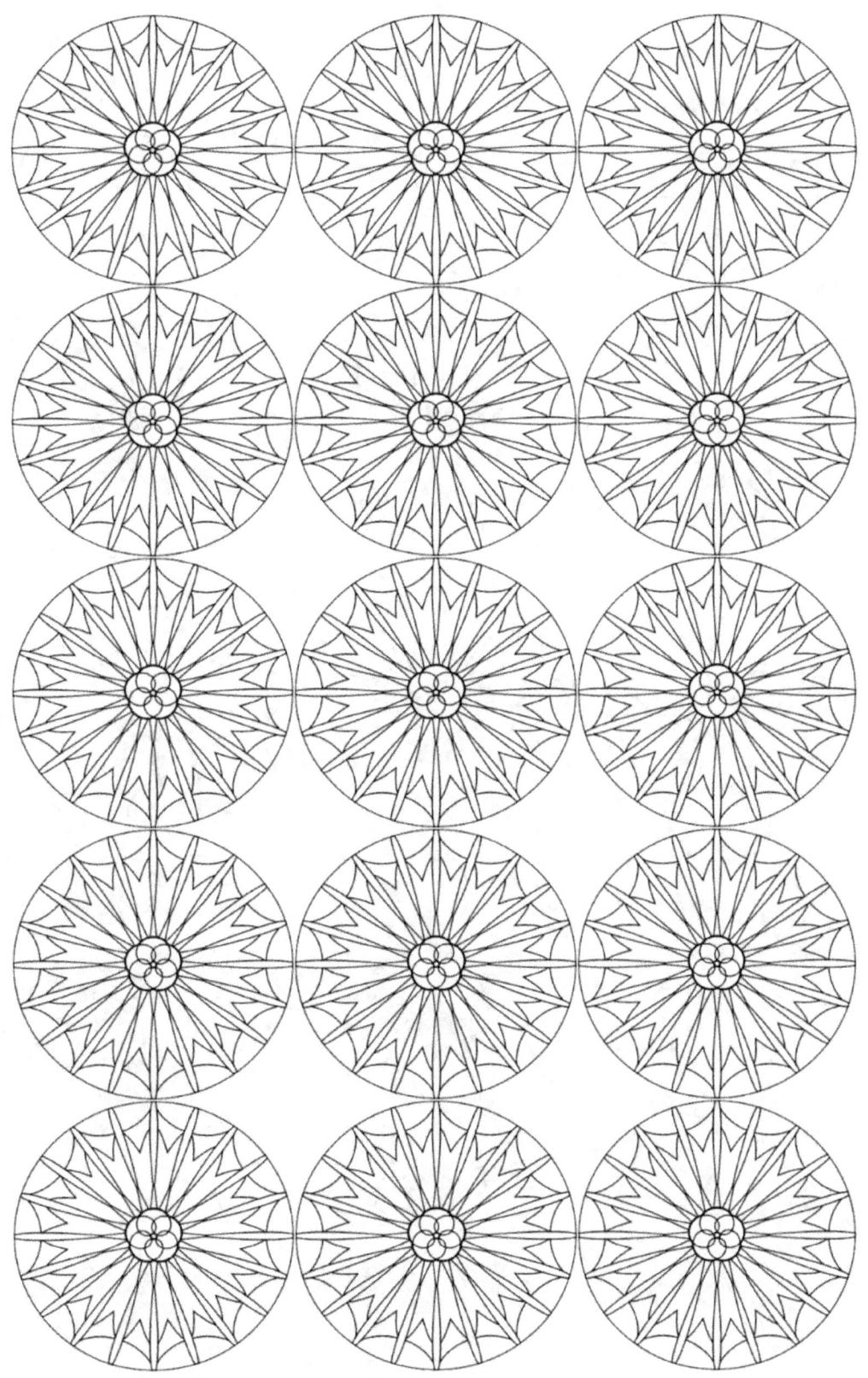

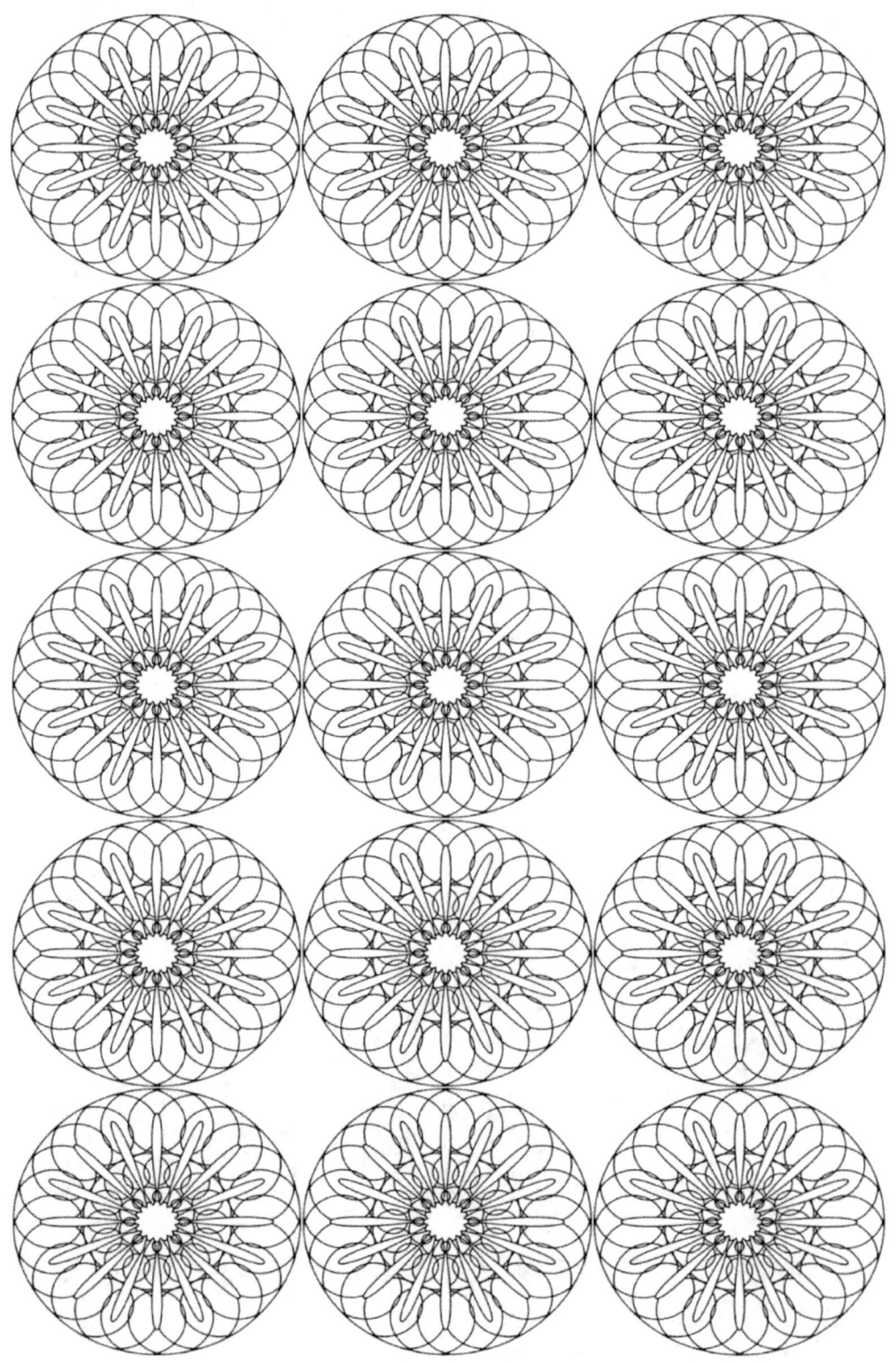

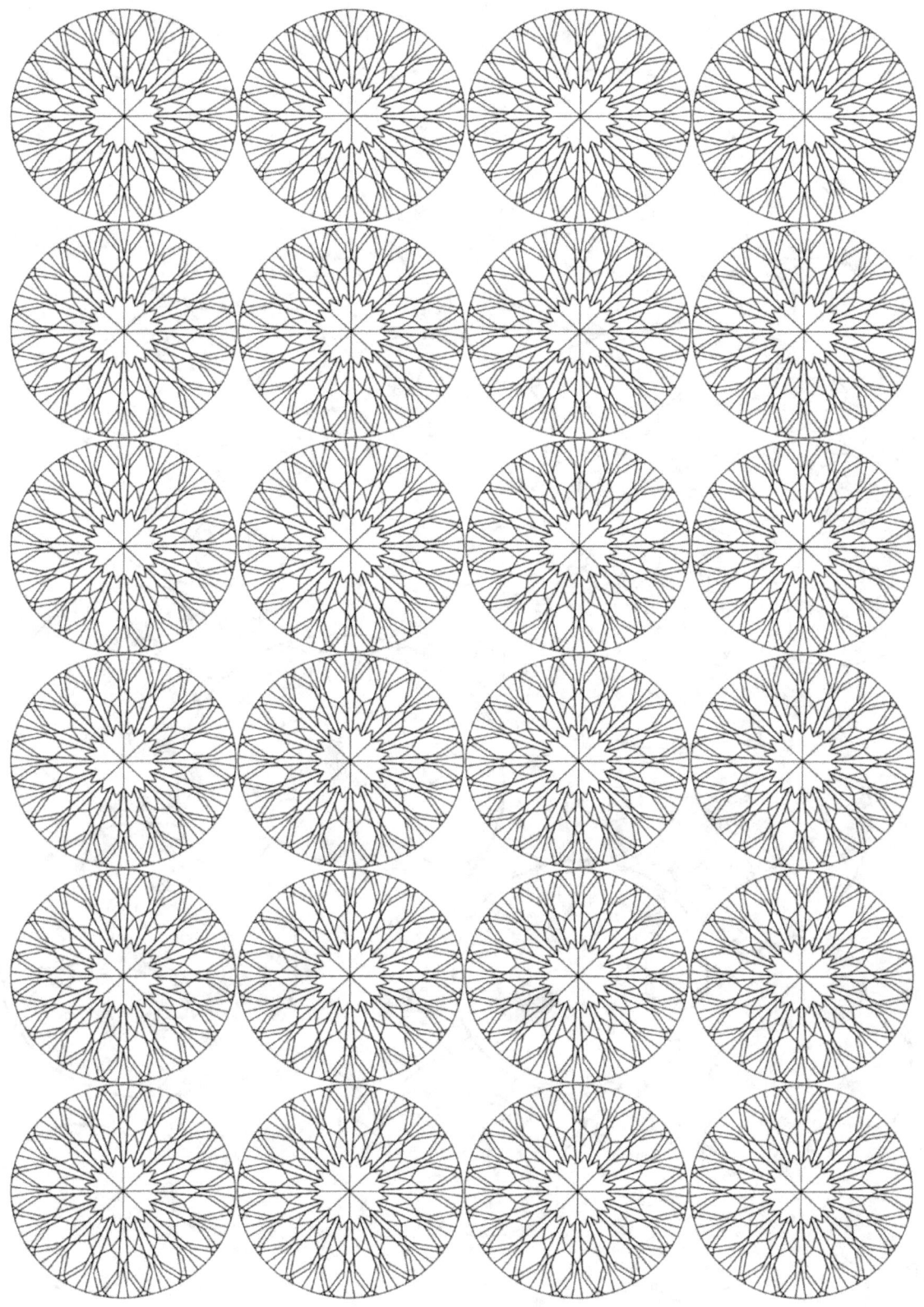

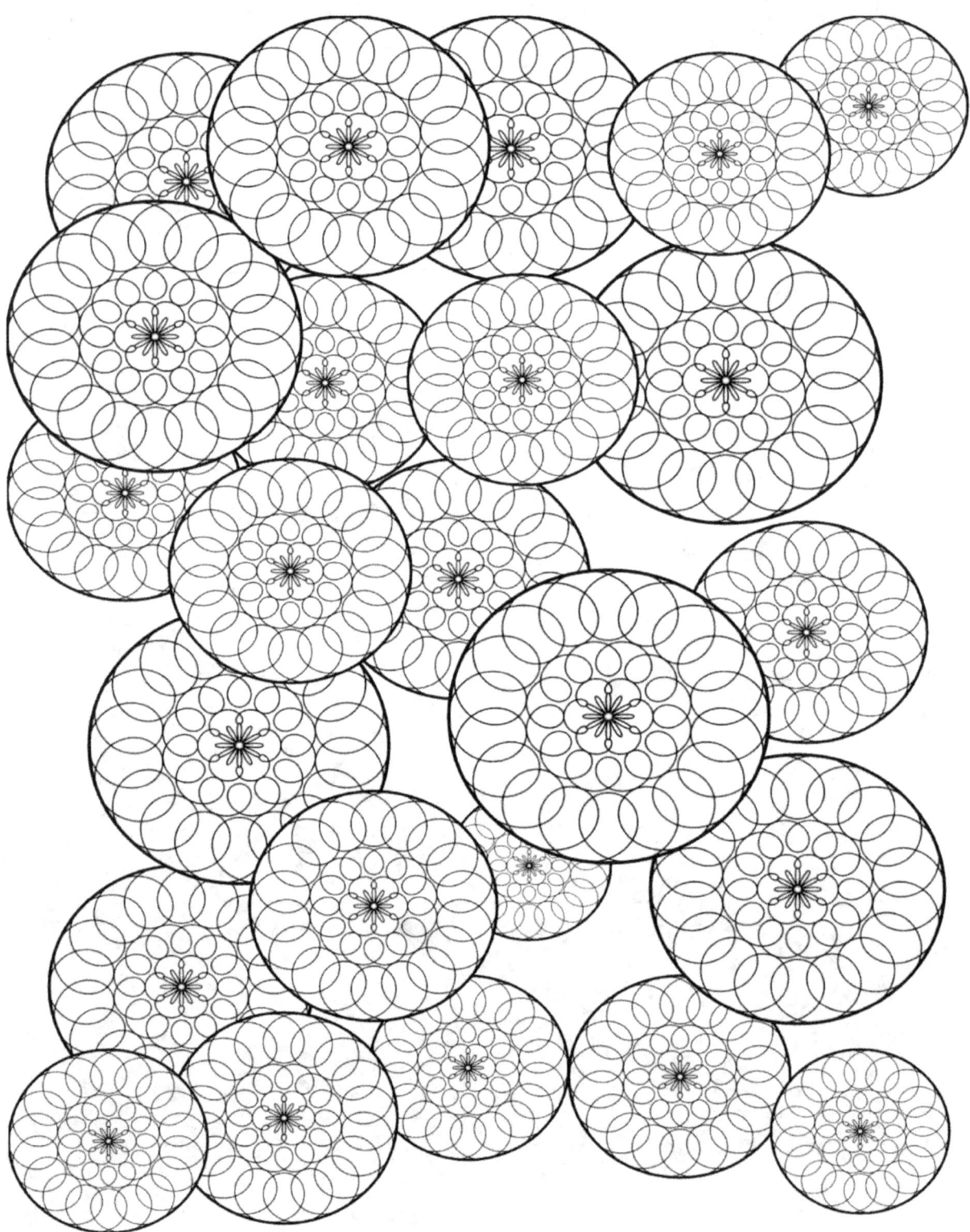

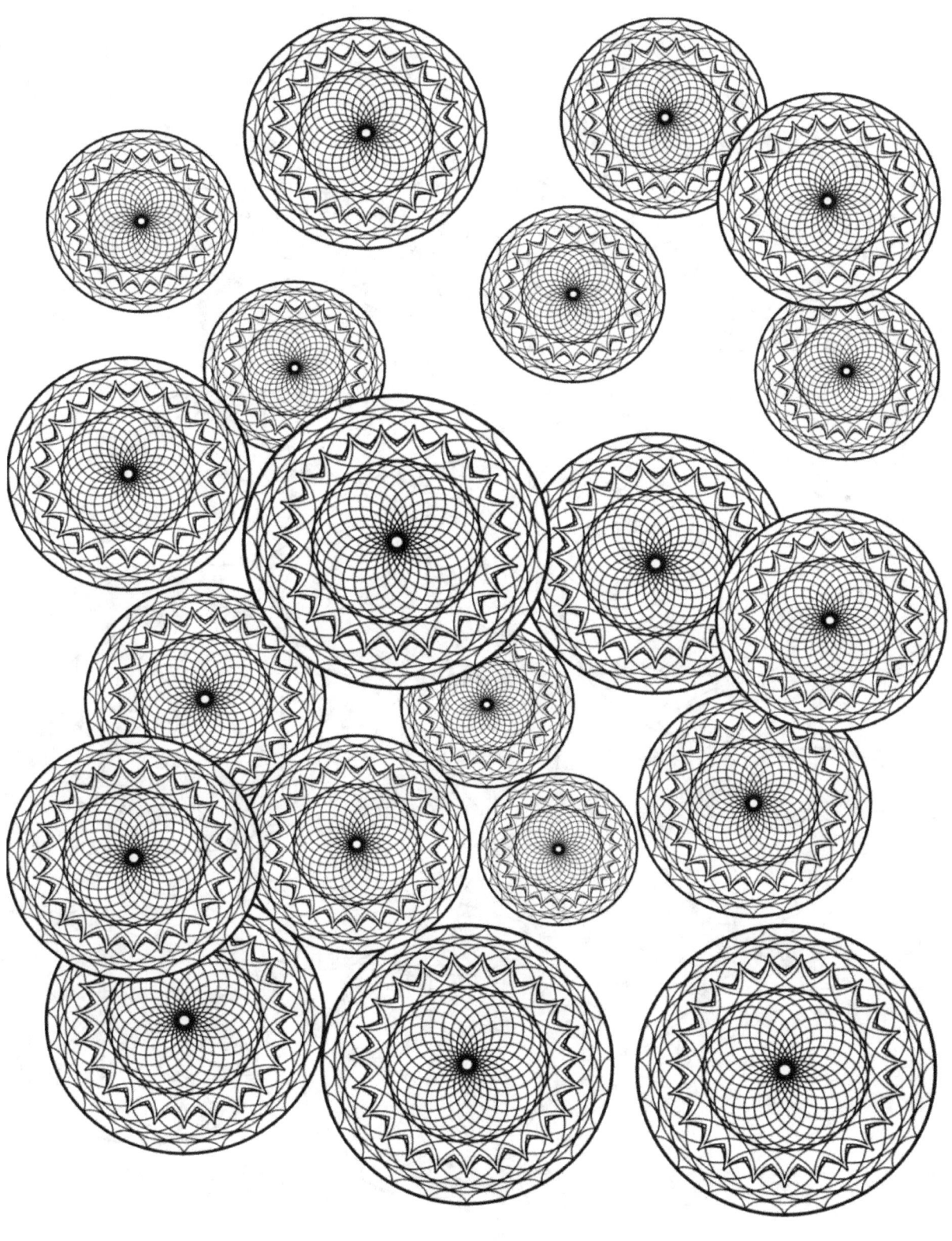

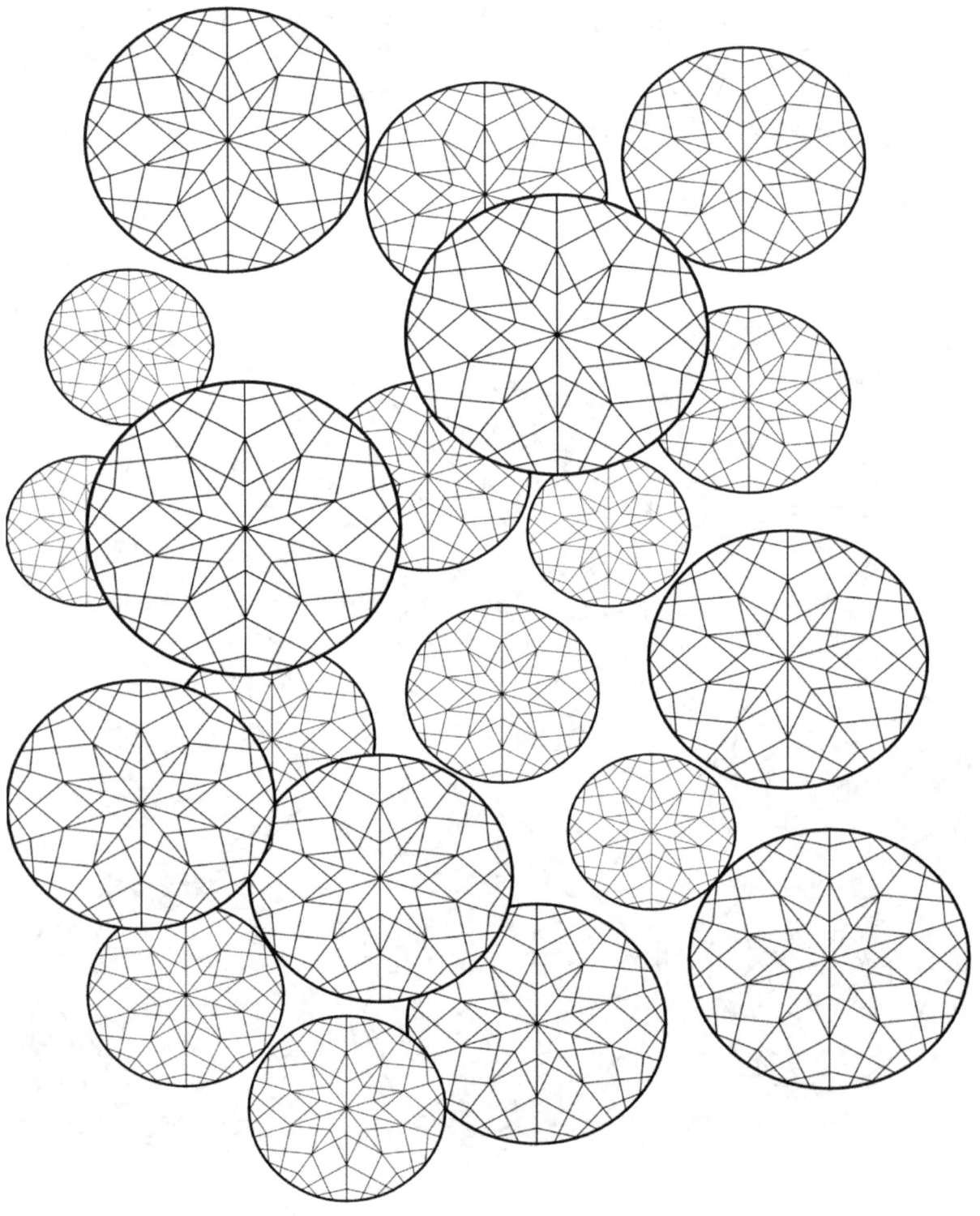

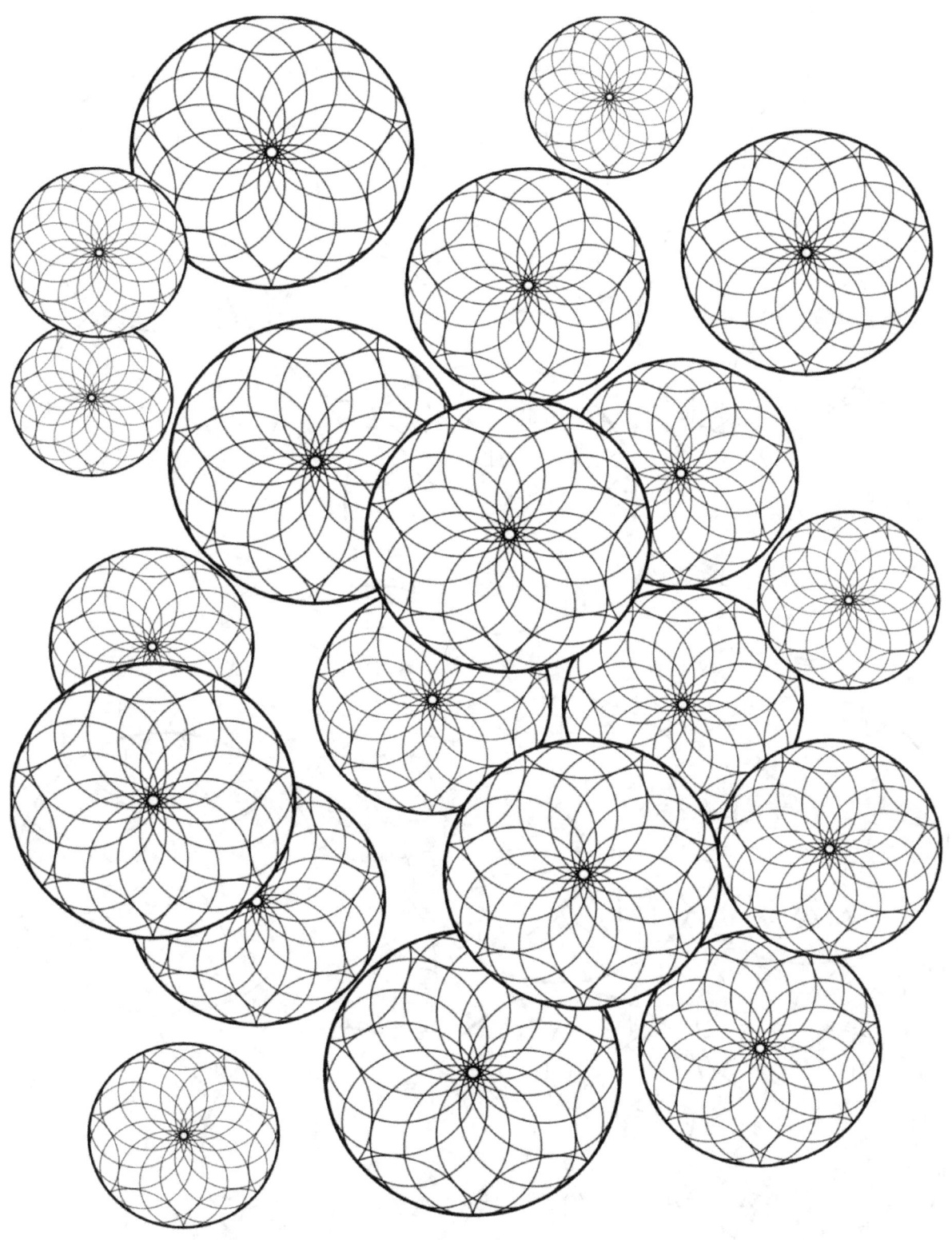

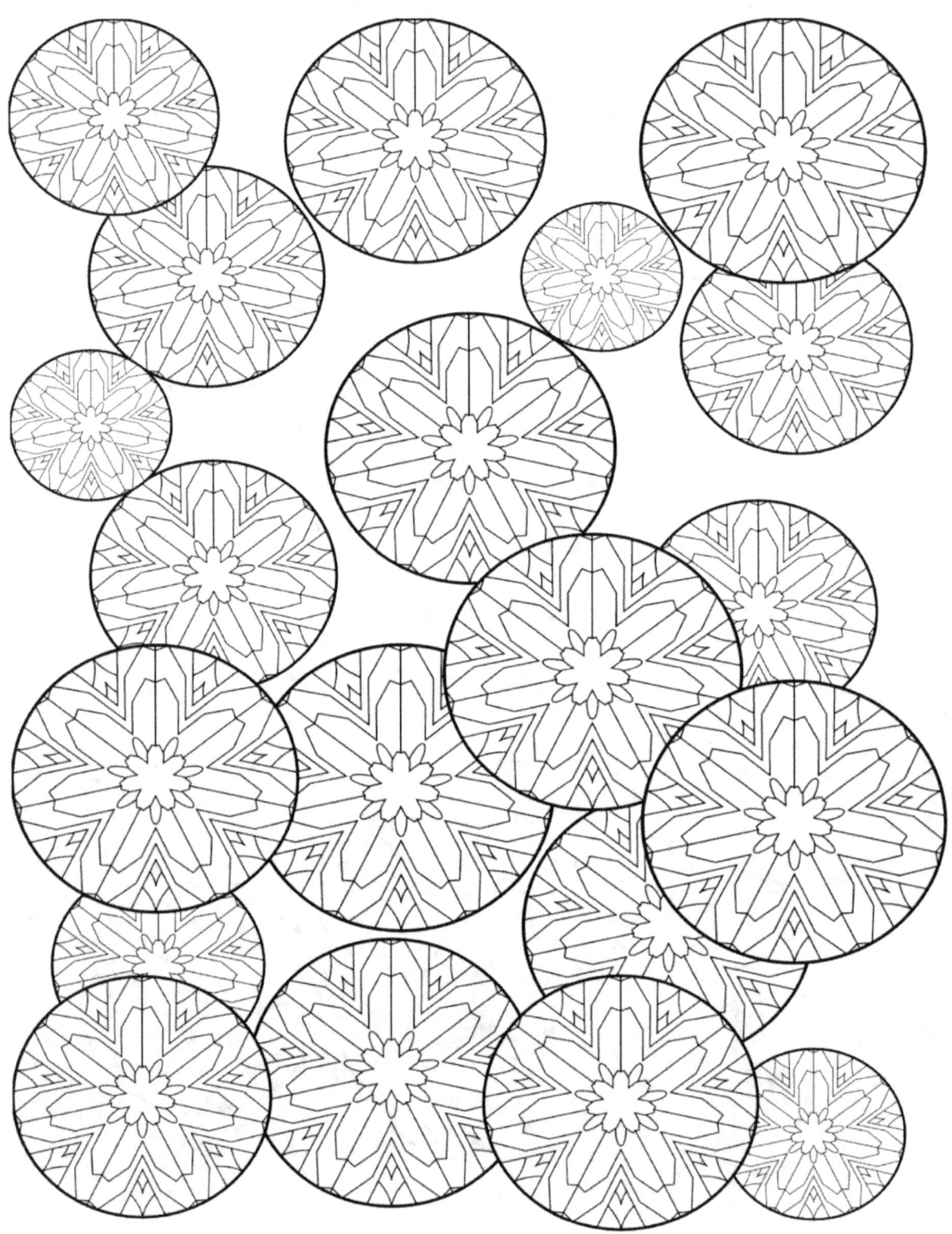

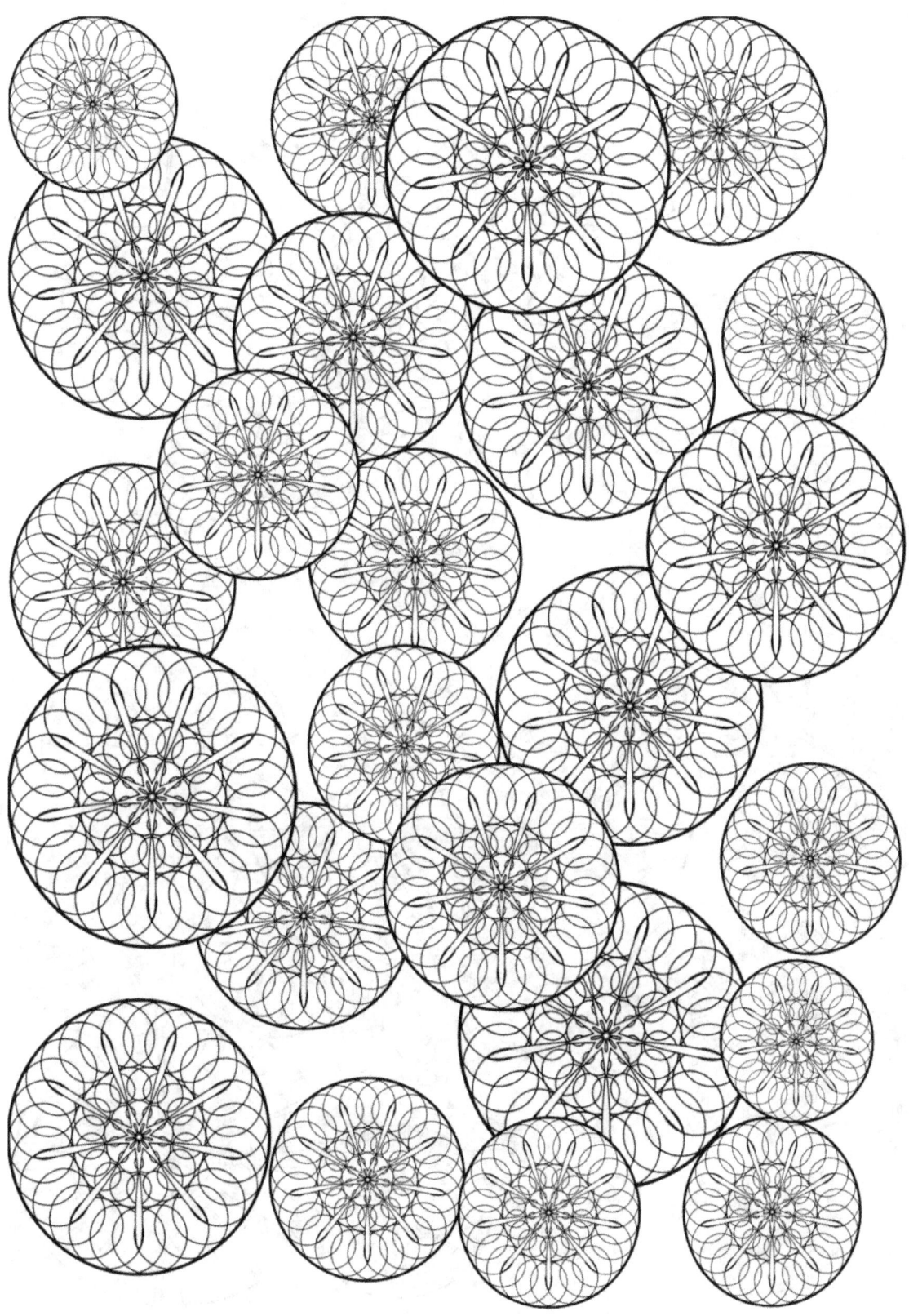

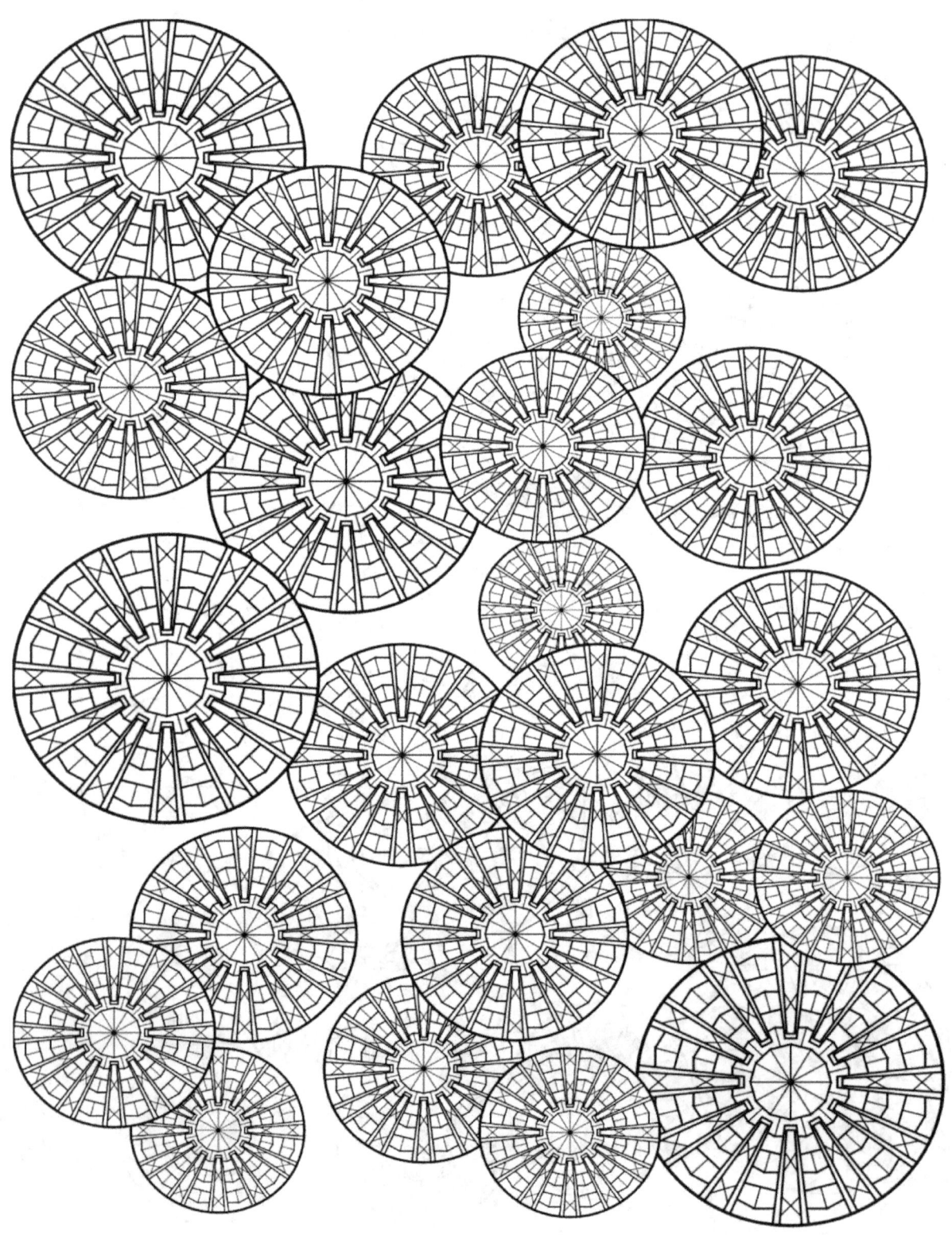

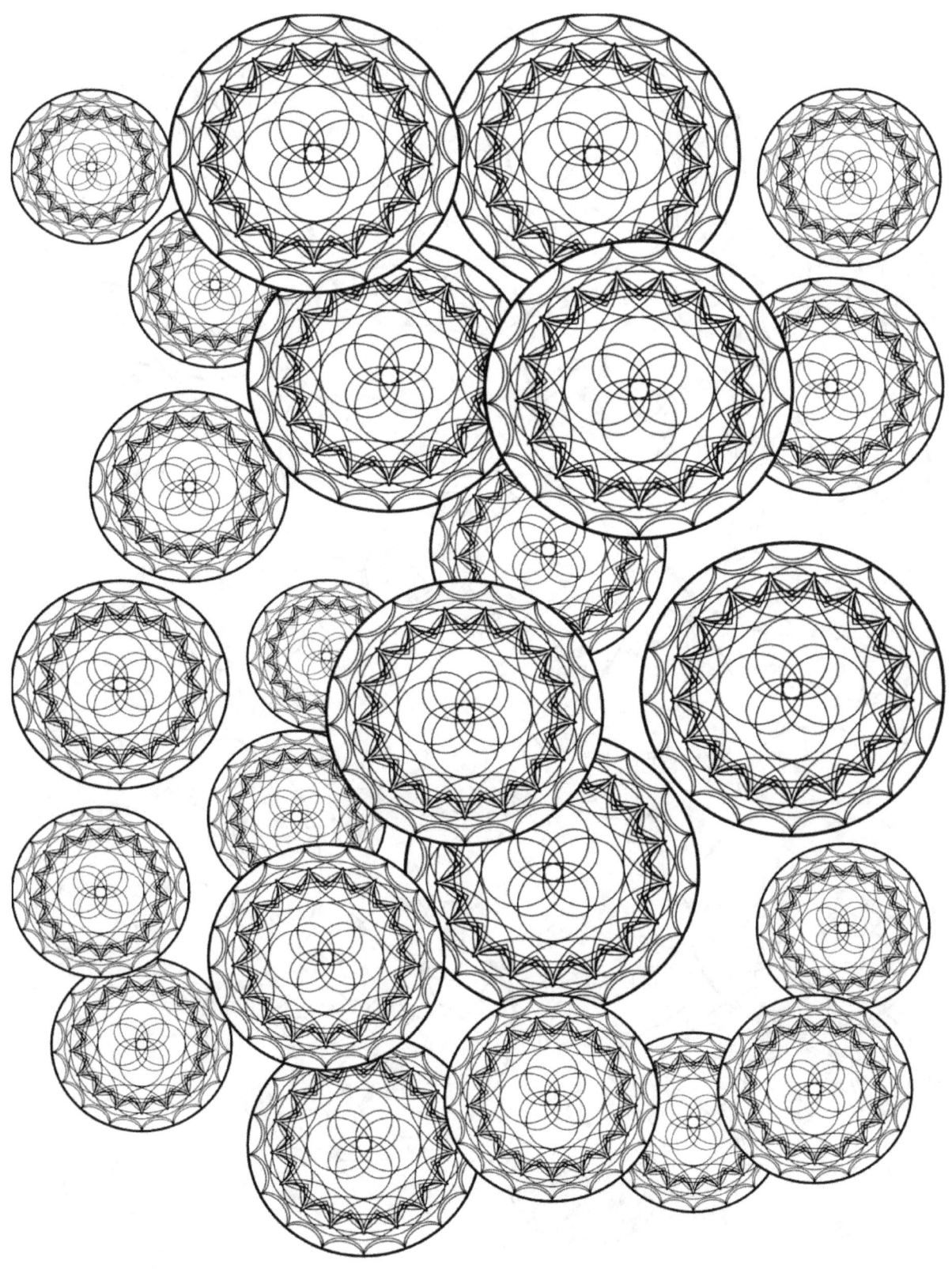

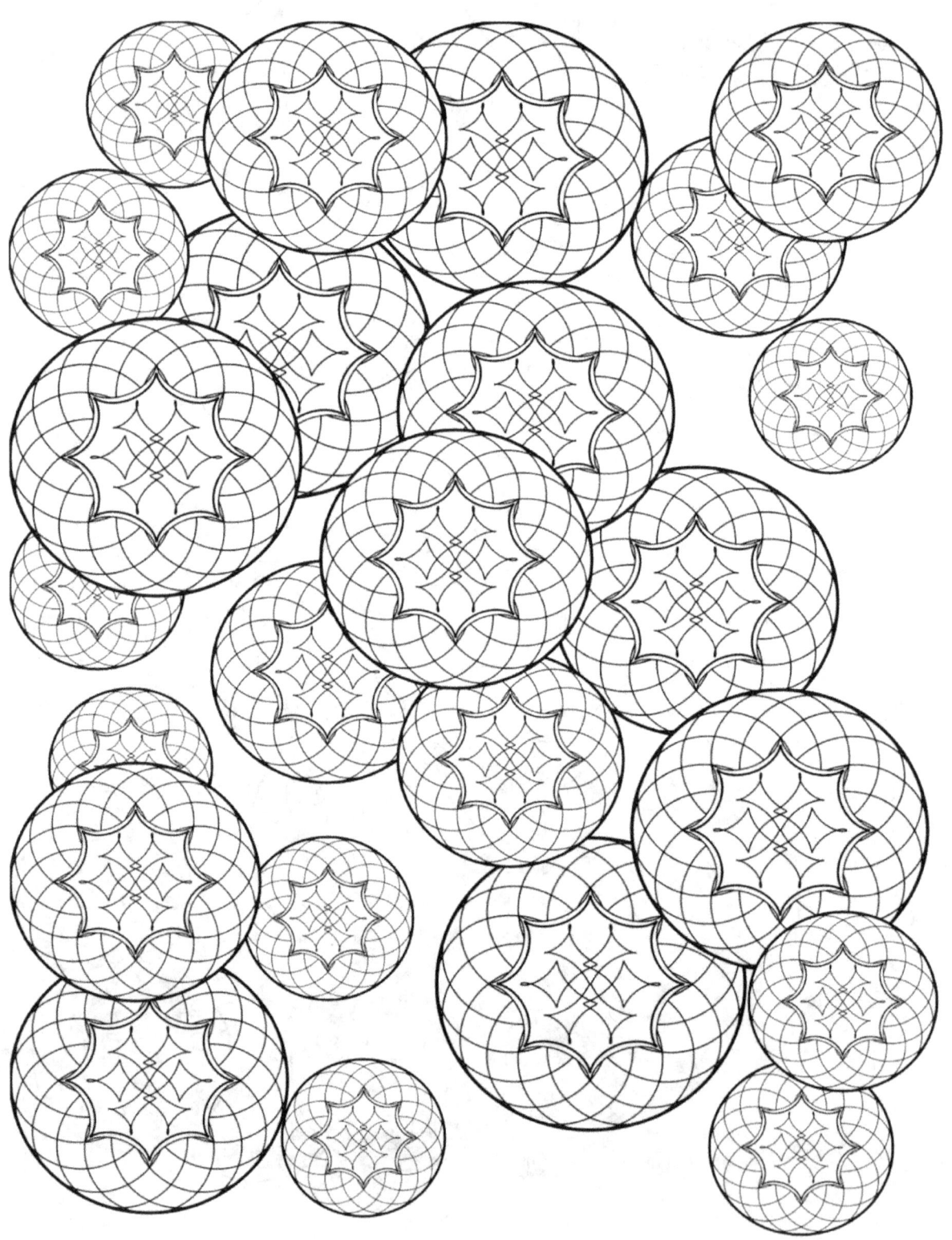

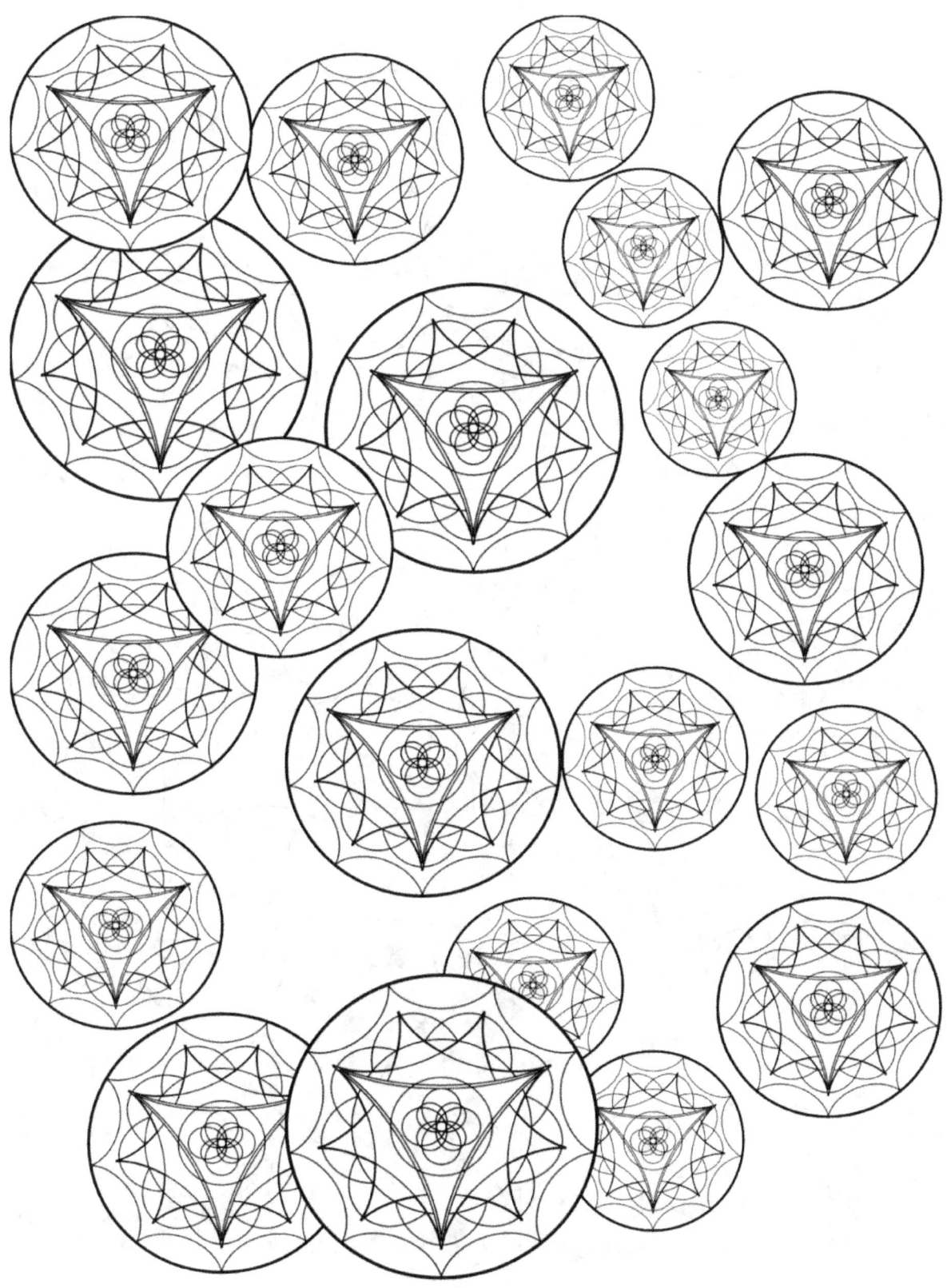

51

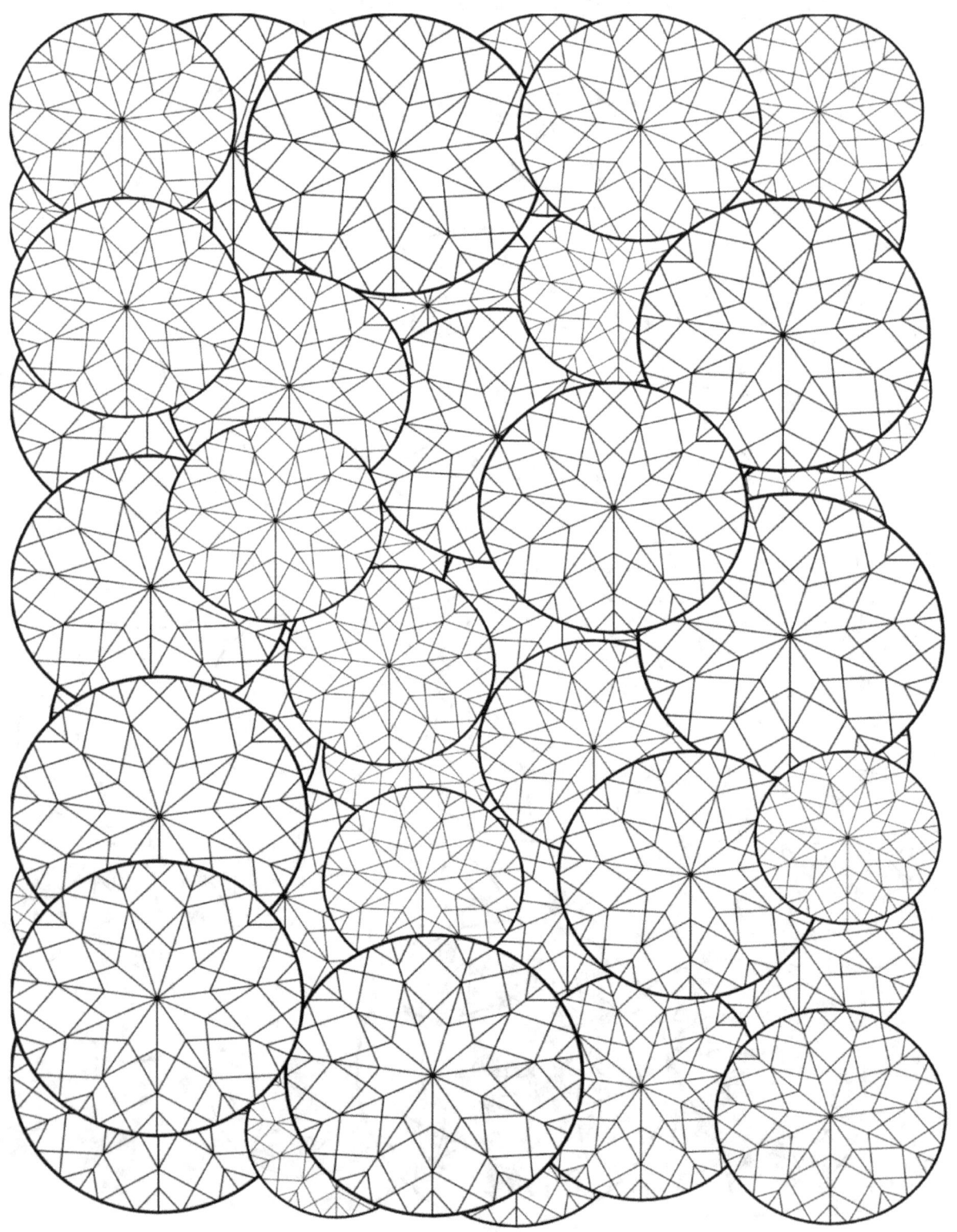

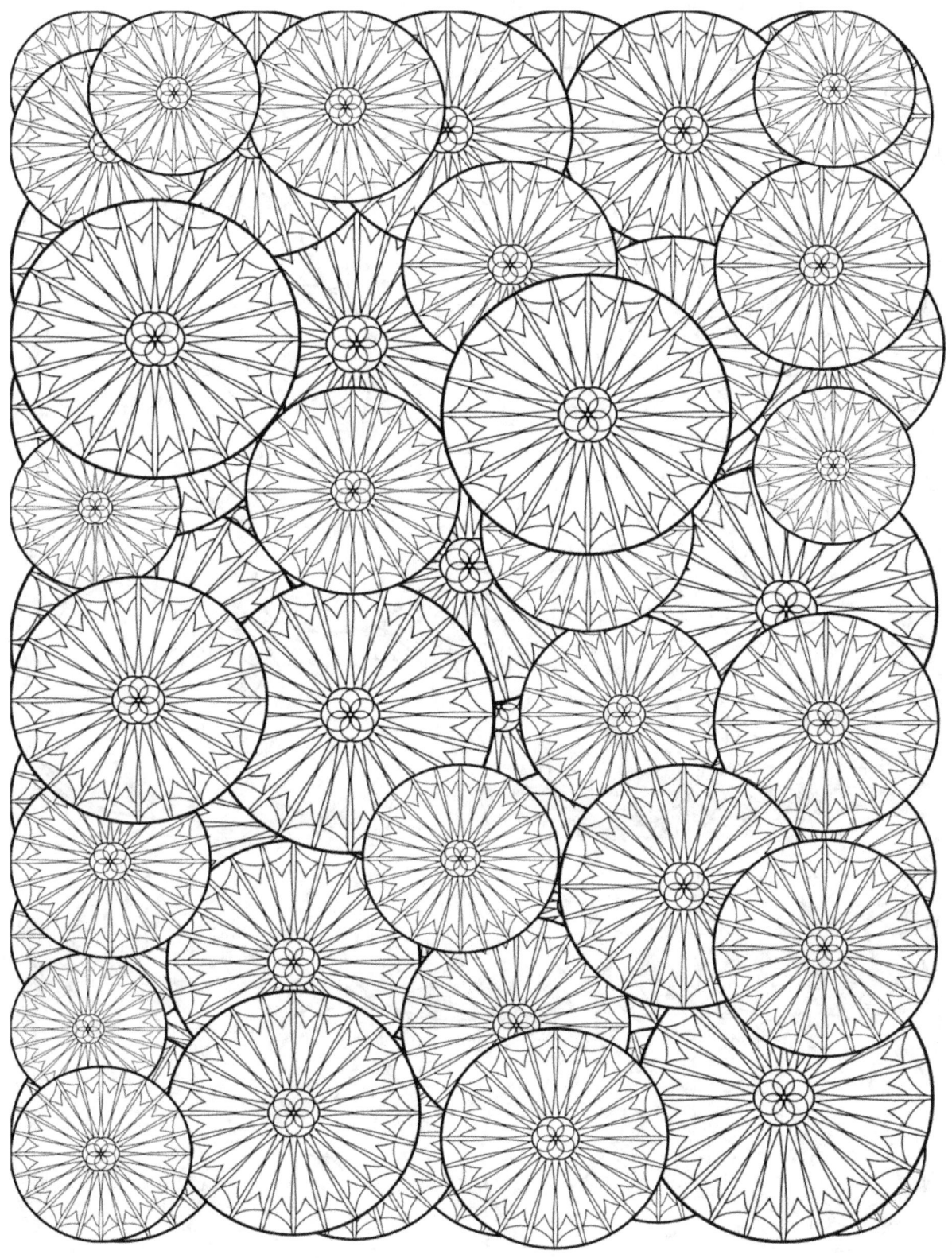

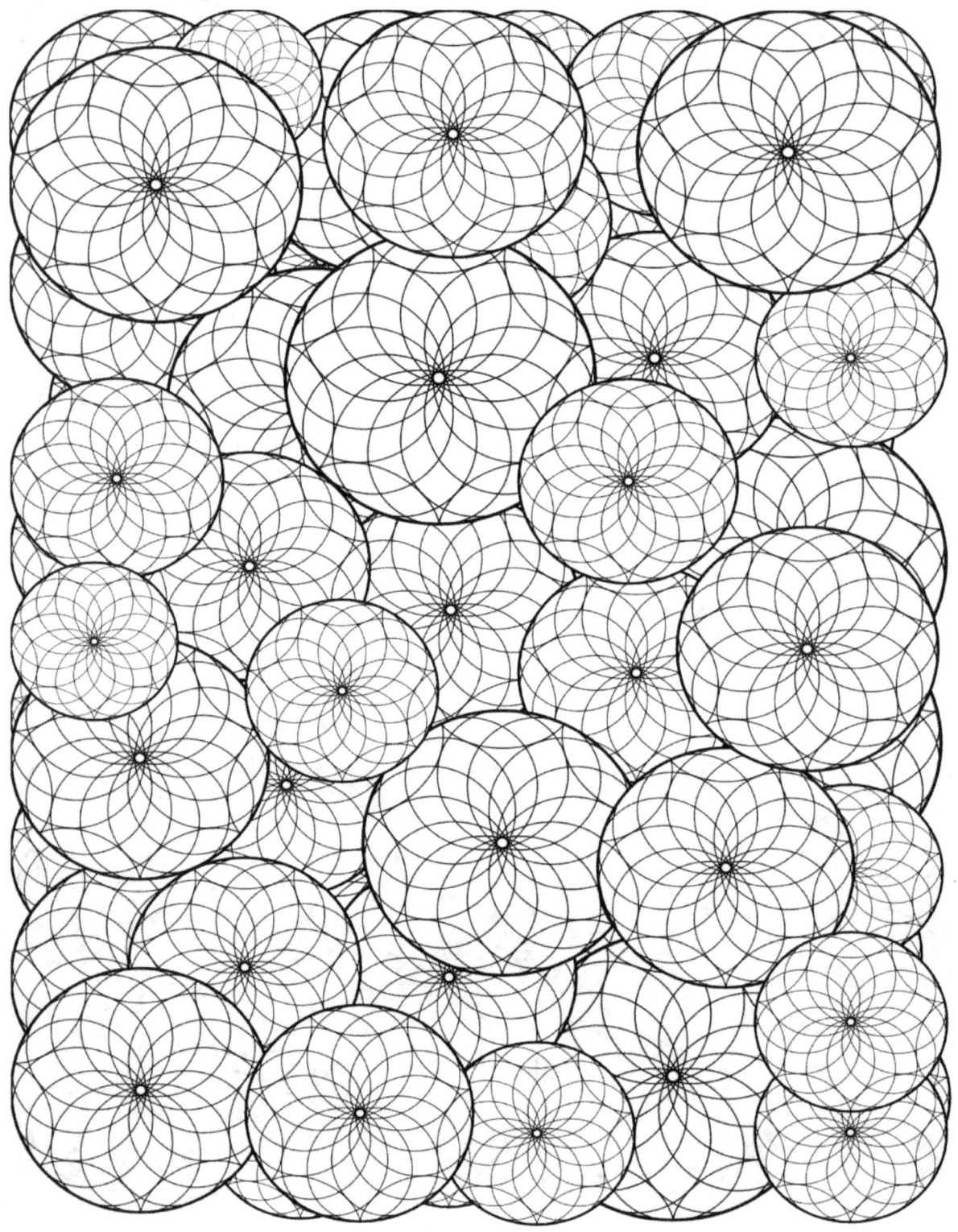

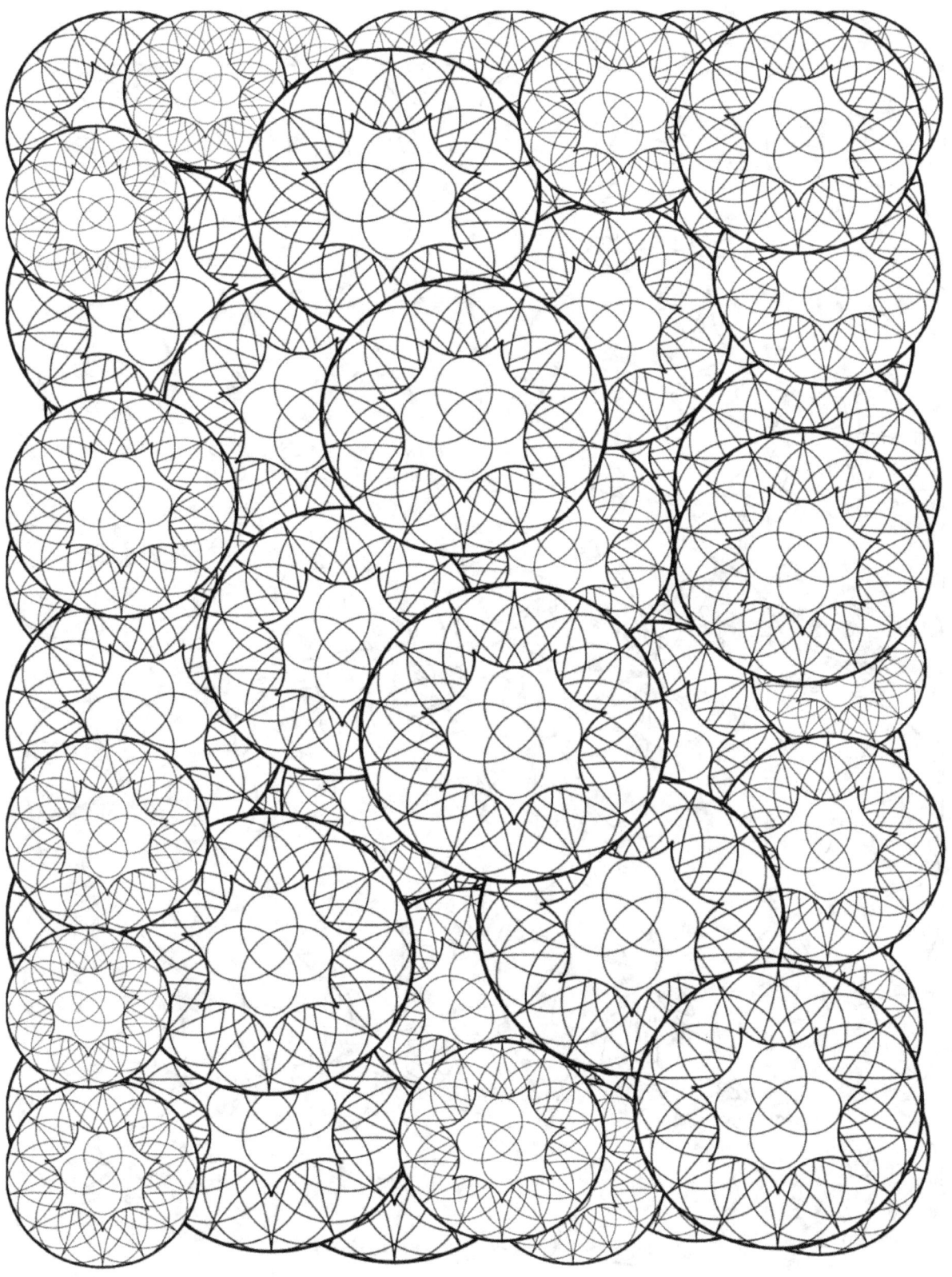

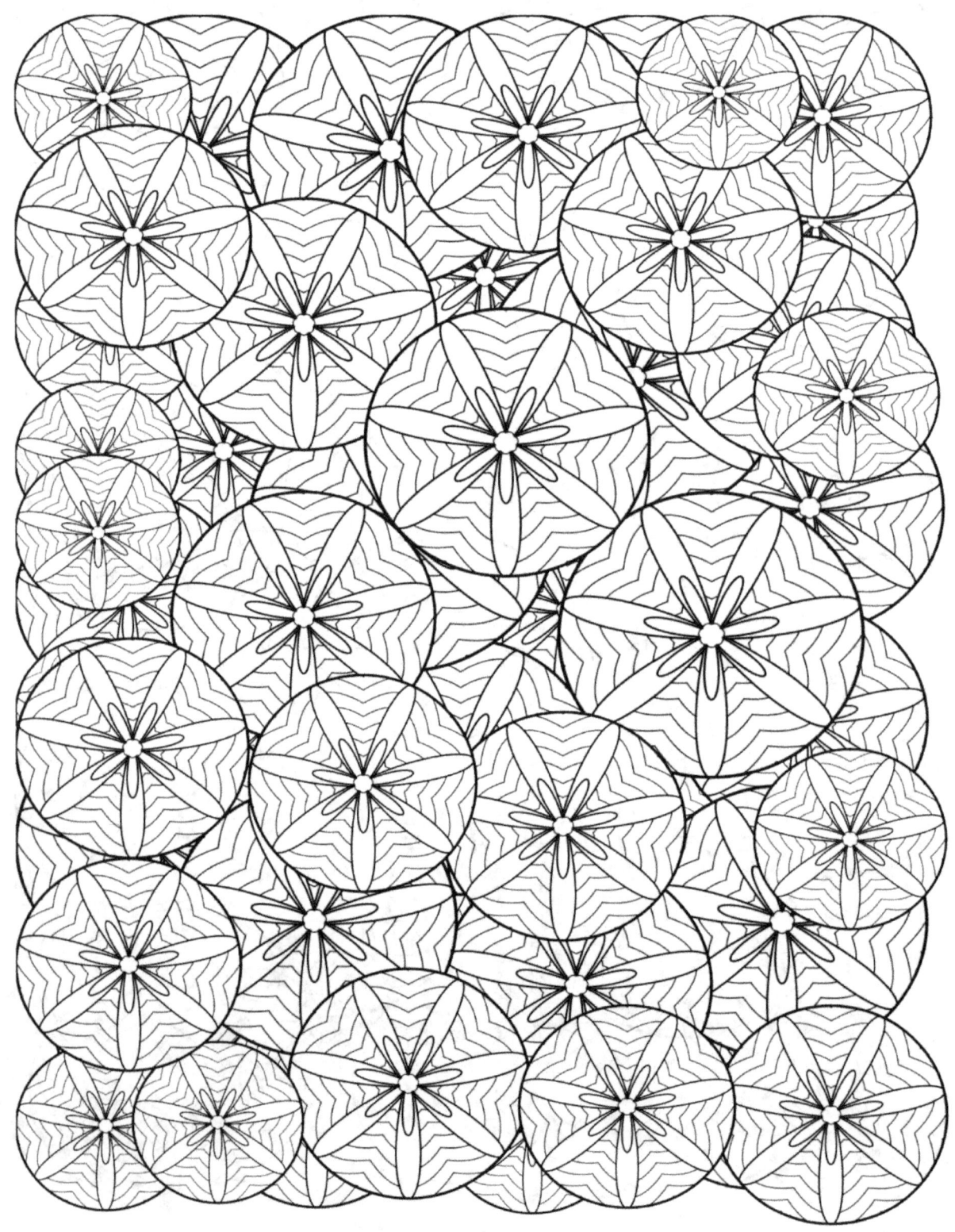

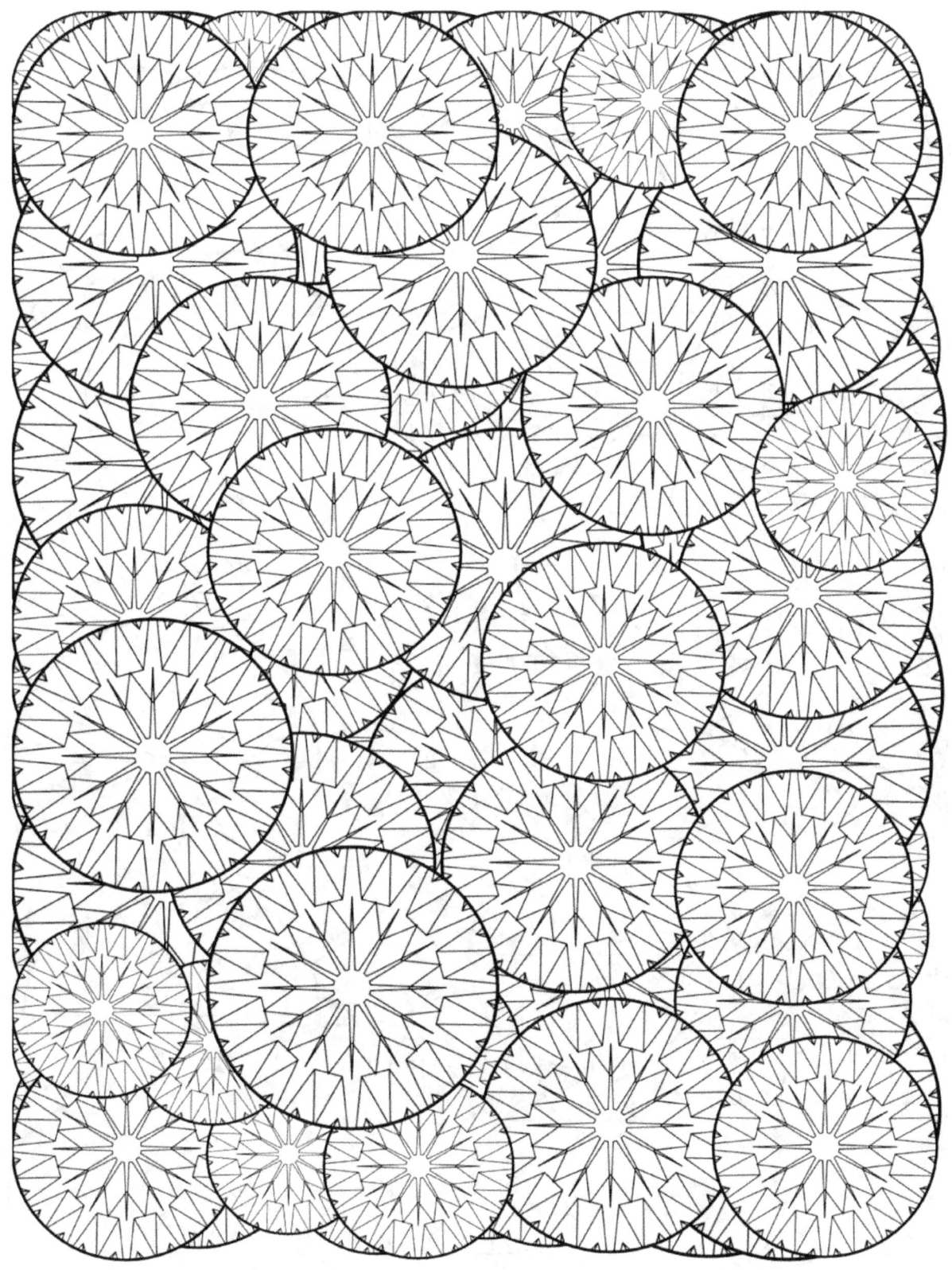

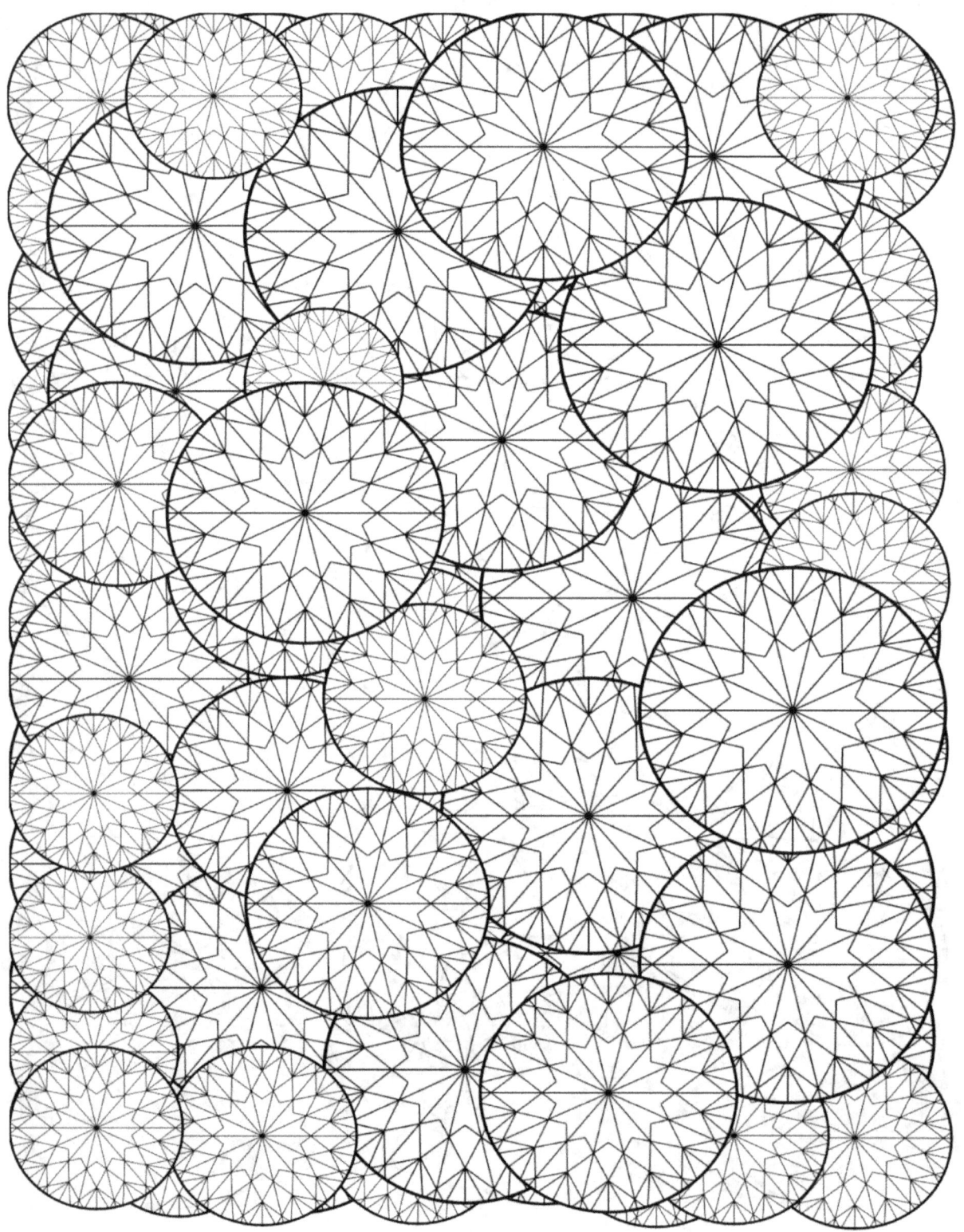

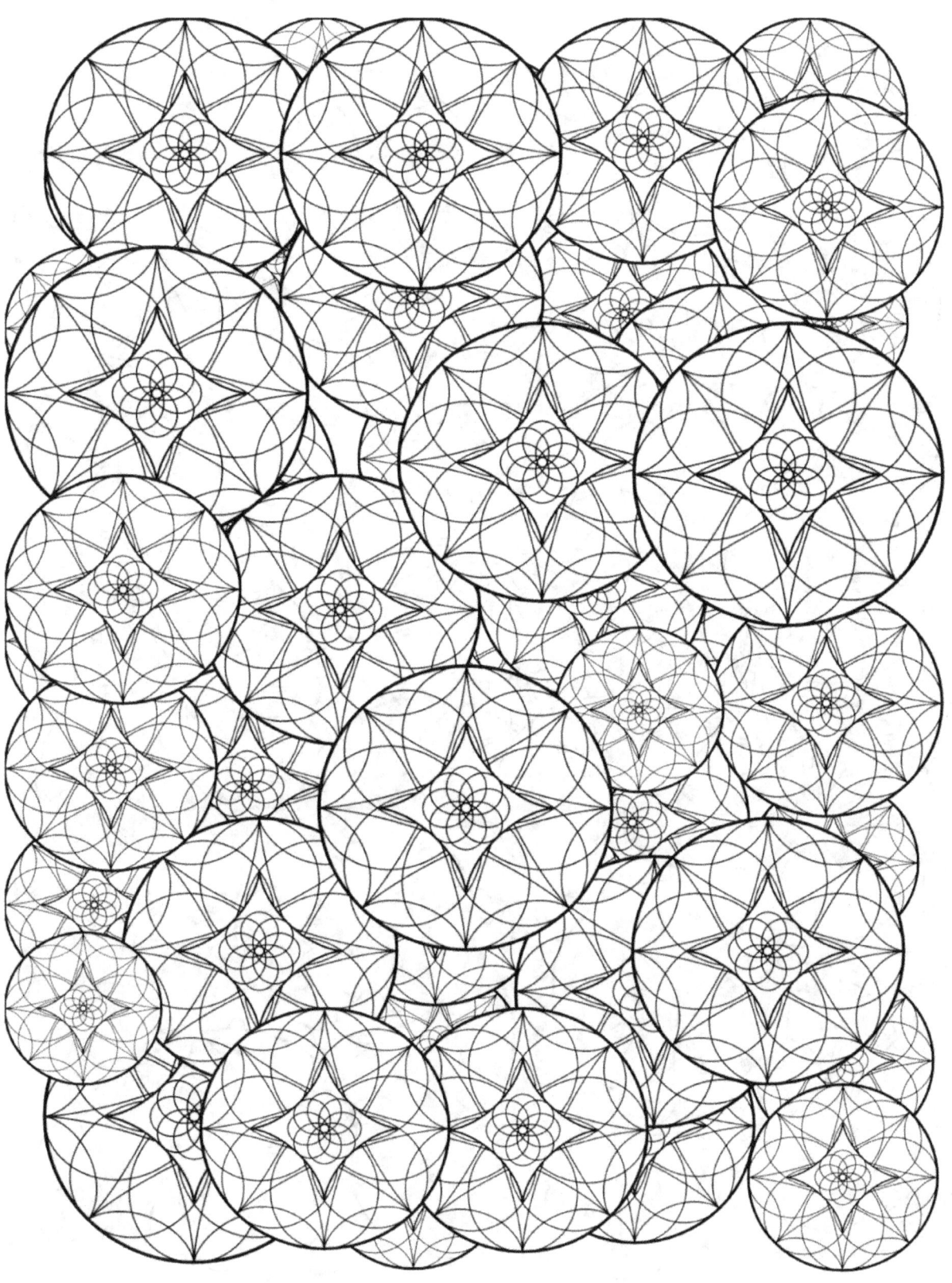

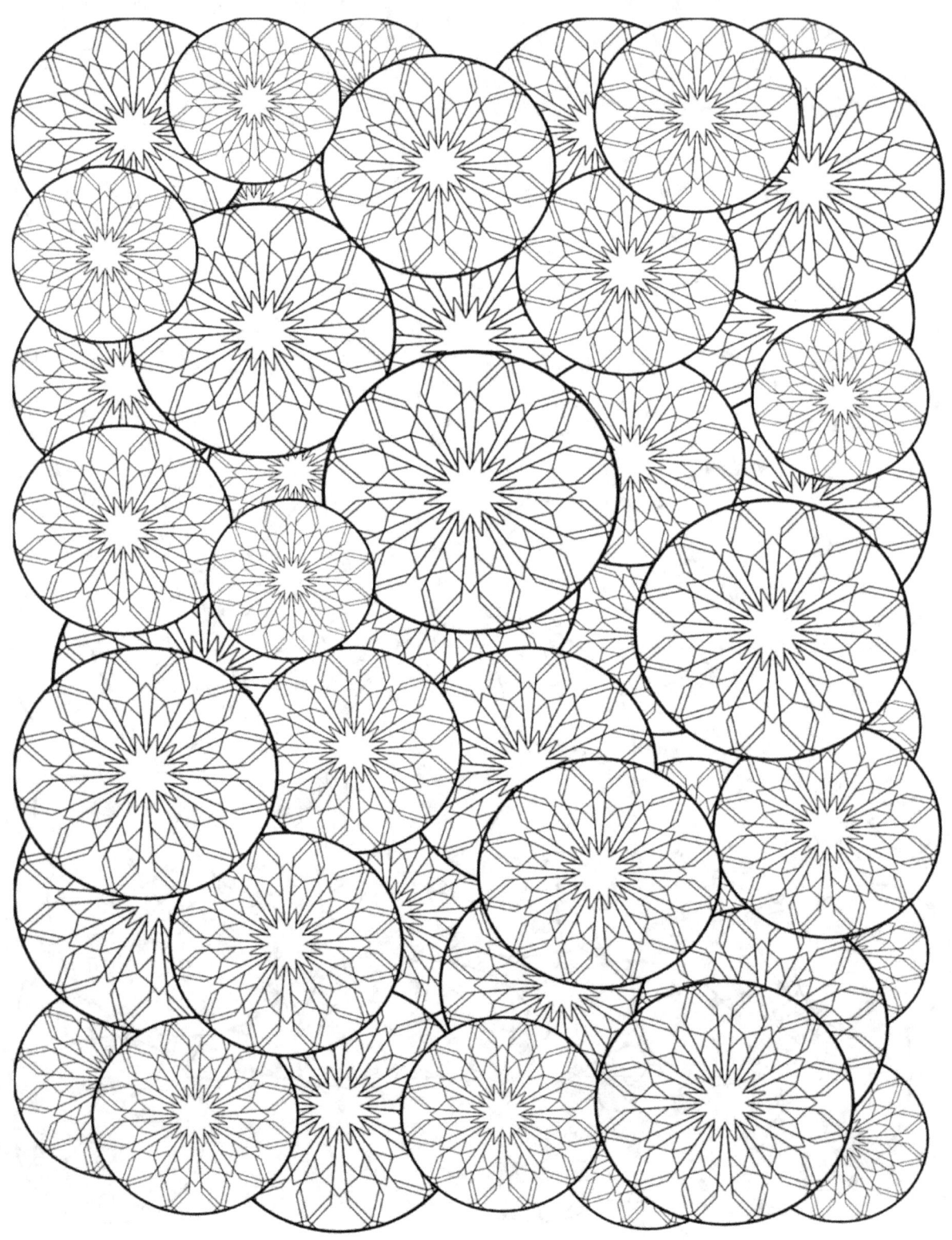

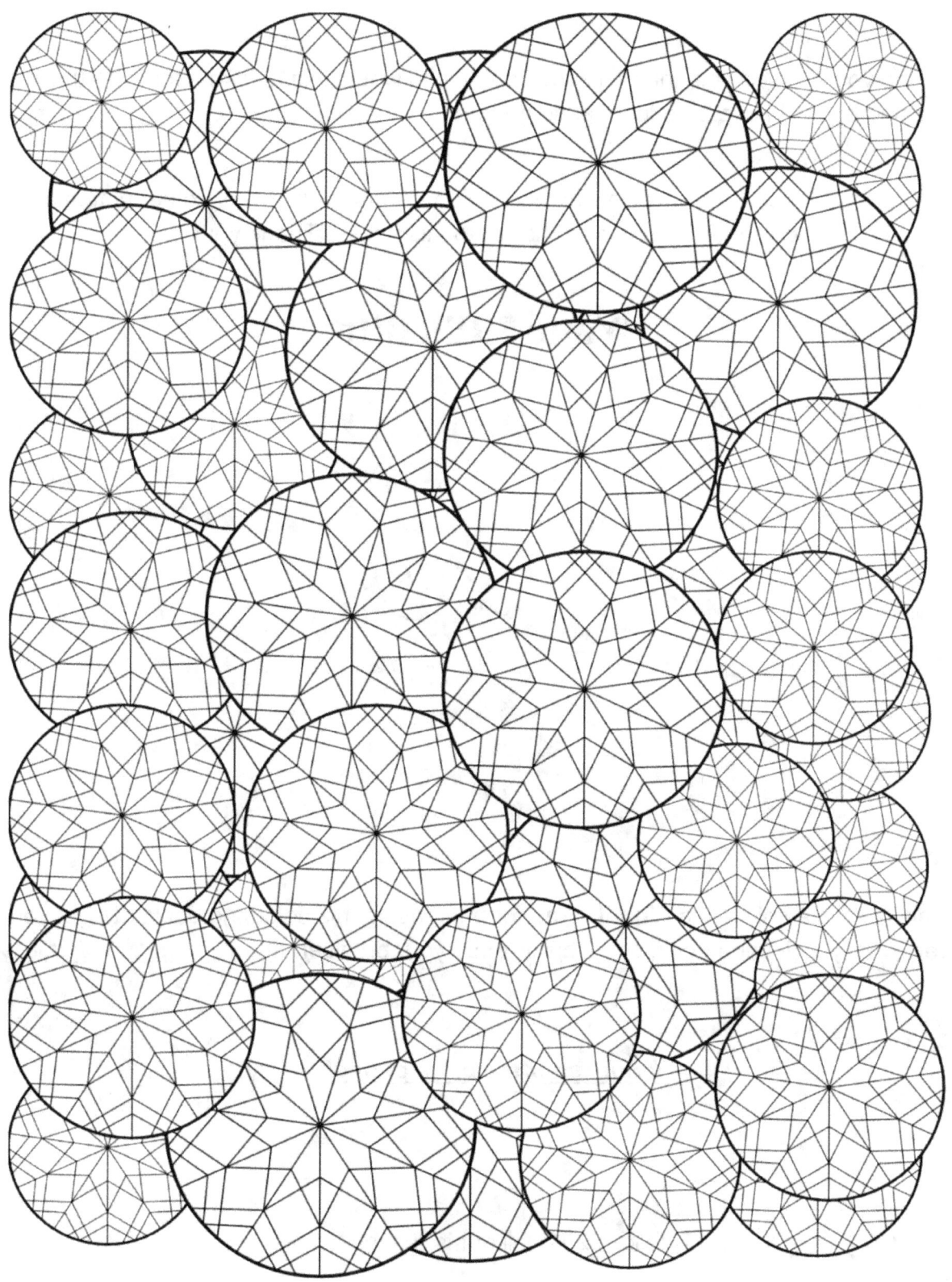

I hope you enjoyed colouring this book and if you would like to take a look at other colouring books I have on offer, please go to my Website... http://mybooksupply.com/

Would you please leave a review of this book on Amazon, they help other potential customers gain some insight to this book... Thank you!

'Your FREE Gift'

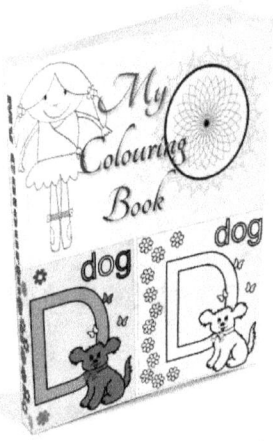

This is my way of saying **'Thank You'** for purchasing this colouring book... to get you Free Family Colouring book, copy this link into your browser... http://eepurl.com/cp50Yz ...

2 books for the price of one!

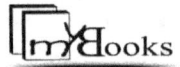

www.ingramcontent.com/pod-product-compliance
Lightning Source LLC
Chambersburg PA
CBHW081255180526
45170CB00007B/2431